791.43

Roger Corman's New World Pictures (1970-1983):

An Oral History

Volume 1

General Editor: Stephen B. Armstrong

Associate Editors: Randy Jasmine, William Nesbitt, Robert Powell

Assistant Editors: Madison Bidinger, Krista Kirkham, Amy Whiting

BearManor
Media

Orlando, Florida

Published in the USA by
BearManor Media
1317 Edgewater Dr. #110
Orlando, FL 32804
www.BearManorMedia.com

Hardcover Edition
ISBN: 978-1-62933-577-3

Printed in the United States of America

Table of Contents

This collection is dedicated to Roger Corman, Jon Davison, Joe Dante and Allan Arkush.

Thanks for the movies.

Introduction

In 1970, following sixteen years of success as an independent motion picture director-producer—with credits including *Attack of the Crab Monsters* (1957), *The Little Shop of Horrors* (1960) and *The Wild Angels* (1966)—Roger Corman launched his own film production-distribution company, New World Pictures. Before selling the company to investors in 1983, Corman would supervise the creation and/or release of more than one-hundred films, among them several features that at once performed well at the box office and addressed important social themes (women's rights, racism, war, the environment): notably *Jackson County Jail* (1976), *I Never Promised You a Rose Garden* (1977), *Piranha* (1978) and *Rock 'N' Roll High School* (1979).

From its inception, New World Pictures attracted ambitious filmmakers who were more interested in gaining practical experience on the set than earning high wages. "At New World, we have a tendency to hire young, talented people," Corman told biographer Ed Naha in 1979. "Young people are aware of this and find their way here.... There's a constant flow of young creative people." Several motion picture directors who began their careers at New World went on to win Academy Awards: Jonathan Demme (*The Silence of the Lambs*, 1991), James Cameron (*Titanic*, 1997) and Ron Howard (*A Beautiful Mind*, 2001).

Corman and his wife, Julie, his producing partner at New World, were also adamant about hiring women filmmakers and many well-known, well-regarded female entertainment figures passed through New World's offices and production spaces. Gale Anne Hurd went on to produce *The Terminator* (1984) and *The Walking Dead* television series; Penelope Spheeris directed the quintessential pop culture comedy *Wayne's World* (1992); and Teri Schwartz became Dean of the UCLA School of Theatre, Film, and Television. As Linda Shayne, who moved into film direction after working on the New World films *Humanoids from the Deep* (1980) and *Screwballs* (1983), told Corman biographer Beverly Gray: "Roger has promoted more women to positions of power than probably any person I know."

While New World primarily produced and distributed genre films—science fiction, crime, horror—Corman and Frank Moreno, his general sales manager, sensed that "prestige pictures would give New World heightened credibility in the market place." As a result, the company in 1972 commenced with an initiative, in Beverly Gray's words, to acquire "art-house release(s) for domestic distribution." Corman's longtime attorney, Barbara Boyle, subsequently served New World as a buyer of high-end films produced abroad, notably Ingmar Bergman's *Cries & Whispers* (1972), which would receive an Academy Award nomination in the Best Picture category. Subsequent to this, Boyle and Corman secured for North American release Fellini's *Amarcord* (1974) and Truffaut's *Small Change* (1977). In addition, New World distributed motion pictures made by maverick independent American filmmakers Melvin van Peebles, Larry Cohen and Andy Warhol, as well as Canadian director David Cronenberg.

The cultural impact of New World Pictures has been enormous as New World alumni Joe Dante (*Gremlins*, 1984) and James Cameron (*Aliens*, 1986), while exploiting storytelling methods passed on to them by Corman, have made some of the most popular films of the past forty years. Corman's willingness to give untested filmmakers the chance to work contributed, in fact, to the Academy of Motion Picture Arts and Sciences' decision to recognize him in 2009 with an Academy Award. A statement produced for this honor declared: "The Academy's Board of Governors voted Corman the Honorary Oscar for his unparalleled ability to nurture aspiring filmmakers by providing an environment that no film school could match."

The films produced by the Cormans under the New World aegis were mostly made on minute budgets with narratives that exploited then-trendy topics ranging from outlaw bikers to swamp monsters and frequently underscored the unseemly, ludicrous and dangerous aspects of American culture, e.g., the sadism that seeps through professional sports; the pervasiveness of sexual violence against women; the unending divisions between the gentry and the poor; and systemic racism. In addition, the majority of the New World films made for Corman share distinct thematic markers and tropes regardless of their genre: humor, action, softcore sex and political content.

Greg Villepique in a 2000 profile addresses the manner in which Corman shaped the films made for New World: "As production executive, he retained approval of each film's basic concept (usually he came up with it), script, casting and final cut, so as long as a film's concept was salable to theaters, as long as it contained plenty of thrills, chases, humor and (starting in the '70s) breasts, he was happy to pay a novice director practically nothing to learn on the job." Corman allowed, even encouraged, left-leaning themes and sympathies to permeate the films. Villepique notes: "Though he maintains a very low public profile, he's also declared that he likes to get a politically liberal point of view into his movies, though usually in a vague way: an outsider stands up for his beliefs and sticks it to The Man, who may be a Satan-worshipping prince [or] a buxom prison matron." Yet Corman has long repudiated the notion that he is a producer-auteur of the sort exemplified by, say, Walter Wanger, Stanley Kramer or Val Lewton as he regards filmmaking as the most collaborative medium in commercial entertainment. The consistency with which the New World films made under his supervision exploit sex, action, comedy and left wing political messaging is the result, that is, of Corman's creative decrees *and* the freedom he permitted his employees as they interpreted these decrees.

We find an example of this dynamic working itself out in the production history of one of the company's best-remembered releases, *Death Race 2000* (1975). Planned as a science fiction movie in which the heroes helm weaponized racecars and speed across a totalitarian America killing pedestrians for points, *Death Race* had been greenlighted by Corman after United Artists in the summer of 1974 announced that it was going to make *Rollerball* (1975), a dystopian futuristic fantasy about brutal roller derby skaters. Chris Petit and Tony Rayns explain, "*Death Race 2000* was dreamed up as a quickie rival to *Rollerball*, and it was apparently Corman himself who had the idea of exploiting United Artists' lumbering multimillion-dollar project by producing a cut-price, low-budget alternative."

Director Paul Bartel was told that he would need to cast, shoot and cut the movie in less than a year, for which he would receive $5 thousand. Bartel rejected the first version of the script Corman presented him, however: "It was extremely unpleasant, very bizarre. The violence was not leavened by much humor and what little humor there was...seemed to be rather forced." Corman okayed a rewrite and gave the script to Charles B. Griffith—a longtime associate who'd crafted the scripts for Corman's *A Bucket of Blood* (1959) and *The Little Shop of Horrors* (1960) and who subsequently directed the New World releases *Eat My Dust!* (197 6) and *Up from the Depths* (1979). "Chuck added a human touch, and a lot of humor, which was also my principal interest," Bartel said. To make the film's characters and their approaches to killing pedestrians less barbaric, the director insisted on muting the narrative's violence paradoxically by amplifying it. "[T]he whole idea of inflicting death more or less capriciously seemed to me a good basis for comedy," Bartel explained to Michael Singer. "[T]he only way I could deal with it was to exaggerate it outrageously, artificialize it."

Corman for the most part kept away from the shoot, instead reviewing the dailies at New World's offices. Though Bartel's farcical take on the subject matter annoyed Corman, he ultimately permitted the director to cut the film himself with editor Tina Hirsch. Yet Corman also insisted upon having several overtly comic sequences left out and had Chuck Griffith and Lewis Teague, a young editor at New World, shoot and incorporate new material that was bloodier than Bartel's. Bartel himself was not happy with these changes, but in the end he reluctantly endorsed them: "The finished film," he told Michael Singer, "is very much a synthesis of his vision and mine. And people seem to enjoy the film, so I'm not unhappy with it." *Death Race*'s successful marriage of kitsch and polemic—it's critiques of state-sanctioned violence—was not lost on critics. Dave Kehr, who recognized and valued the movie's structural, thematic and aesthetic tensions, declared, "*Death Race* is a first-class piece of agitprop, done up in a bright, flat, comic-book style, that effectively forces the critical viewer to make hard, personal decisions about what is and what is not acceptable as 'catharsis.'"

Films such as *The Lady in Red* (1979), *Piranha*, *Jackson County Jail* and *Galaxy of Terror* (1981) similarly rise above the silliness of low-budget exploitation pictures produced by other production groups during the same period. Yet the New World output by and large has been ignored by the critical establishment because so many of the films made for the company are works of fantasy and science fiction, which academic critics still rank low in the hierarchy of movie genres. Corman, notably, grew up reading and watching science fiction entertainment and has never himself considered it a secondary or lesser category of work. And through his own career as a director-producer prior to New World's founding, he made many outstanding stories about weird monsters and confrontations with alien forces and the like, among them *It Conquered the World* (1956), *Not of This Earth* (1956) and *Creature from the Haunted Sea* (1961). In a 1957 manifesto he published on the topic of sci-fi, Corman argued that stories about outer space and the technology of tomorrow could achieve the same aesthetic heights as more standard fare if writers and directors learned to differentiate "between the over-contrived science fiction feature which recapitulates all of the clichés of its category and the truly original, soaring feature."

Corman would find intelligent sci-fi stories of this sort just two years later when Rod Serling's *The Twilight Zone* TV series premiered on CBS in 1959. Serling realized that he could insert edgier material inside the science fiction and weird tales that made up *Twilight Zone* as advertisers, sponsors and censors paid less attention to sci-fi than to straight drama productions. Corman soon reached a similar conclusion. And after the commercial failure of the anti-segregation drama *The Intruder* in 1962, he went on to make direct and produce genre films exclusively. His greatest imperative was to ensure these films entertained audiences and, only when possible, delivered critiques of social problems, whatever they may be, obliquely. One of the later films produced and released by New World during Corman's tenure, *Battle Beyond the Stars*, exemplifies this doubleness of purpose, blending commercial appeal and anti-establishmentarian ideals. The loner mercenaries who function as the protagonists in this bit of space opera—modeled after the heroes in Kurosawa's *Seven Samurai* (1974) and Sturges's *The Magnificent Seven* (1960)—all share an obdurate, existential outlook, finding value in the pursuit of survival, if not happiness. As the character St. Exmin declares: "We exist for battle. Out creed is to live fast, fight well and have a beautiful ending." Each of the intergalactic heroes try to survive the way they can—overcoming their own at times reactionary or politically indifferent sensibilities as they strive to save a group of peaceful farmers from bandits, and in doing so allow themes of resistance, revolt and, especially, collective action to refract through the otherwise cartoonish action. The protagonists may not always share the same motivations, but they work together for a common cause, the defeat of a tyrant, who, like Mussolini, Franco or Stalin, uses military power to suppress a population's civil liberties. The heroes' conduct, we might add, exemplifies Corman's own approach to making pictures: "A small band of efficient, dedicated, highly trained warriors can defeat any number of rabble. That's my theory of filmmaking."

A collective effort perpetrated by driven individuals yielded this volume, too, and we'd like to thank the following people and groups for their indefatigable support and generosity: Roger Corman, Julie Corman, Barbara

Boyle, Lisa Reeve, Terry Finn, Jane Ruhm, Frances Doel, Cynthia Brown, Jesse Vint, Steve Carver, Allan Arkush, Joe Dante, Kent Beyda, Mark Helfrich, Jack Hill, Jon Davison, Jonathan Kaplan, Dick Miller, Lainie Miller, Michael Pressman, Paul Chihara, Barry Schrader, Alex Hadju, Linda Spheeris, Lewis Teague, John Sayles, Meredith Atkinson, Belinda Balaski, Mark Goldblatt, Durinda Wood, Sid Haig, Joseph McBride, Larry Bock, Grace Zabriskie, Allan Holzman, David Wall, Jesse Bullington, Susan Justin, Aaron Lipstadt, Alan Toomayan, Adam Walderman, Doug Fowler, Zane Levitt, Martin Kove, *The Production Booth*, Mike White, Rob St. Mary, Logan Geary, Dixie State University IT, April VeVea, Leslie Twitchell, Dixie State University College of Humanities & Social Sciences, Jenn Stewart, Stephen Lee, Dixie State University Library & Learning Services, Dianne Aldrich, Krista Kirkham, Madison Bidinger, Lynzee Horsley, Autumn Nuzman, Megan Hill and Shon Beaumont. Superspecial thanks to Katie Armstrong, MFHD. We have elected to use the spelling of the title of the 1979 New World release *Rock 'N' Roll High School* as it appears in the film's opening sequence; the same spelling shows up on the picture's well-known lobby poster; thanks to JD, AA, KB and MH for their insights.

THE EDITORS

Lobby poster for *Rock 'N' Roll High School* (New World Pictures, 1979).

Interviews

ROGER CORMAN

Interview by Stephen B. Armstrong

STEPHEN B. ARMSTRONG: What was it that prompted you to create New World Pictures? Before the company's launch, you'd had some difficulties with American International Pictures, with *G-a-s-S-S-S* (1970), for instance. And then *Von Richthofen and Brown* (1971) for United Artists. You'd been disappointed by how these movies were handled?

ROGER CORMAN: Yes. The last few films I made for AIP—they did some editing on each. This was the 1960s, the days of the counterculture. I was growing more radical, and they were growing more conservative. On *The Wild Angels* (1966), which was the most successful picture they'd ever had, they cut out certain scenes that they felt were too radical for the audience. They then did the same thing on *The Trip* (1967), and they did the same thing on *G-a-s-S-S-S*.

On *Von Richthofen*, there was a question of accents. I said to the people

at United Artists before making the picture that "The English squadron—
the Brown squadron—will have English accents. Now, for the German
squadron we have a choice. We can play them with German accents, or they
can speak straight English because Germans don't speak German with a
German accent. They just speak German. We can go either way, but we have
to make a decision." We made the decision to have the German squadron
speak American English. When the picture was finished there was a first cut
I showed them. They liked the film, but they said, "Everything is fine. But we
have got to have German accents on the German squadron," which meant
every member of the German squadron and everybody else in Germany
had to have German accents. This was completely opposite to the previous
agreement and, I felt, damaged the performances. At that point, I decided to
start my own production-and-distribution company, New World.

I'd had other difficulties with American International. *The Wild Angels*
and *The Trip*, particularly, were very big successes. AIP had always been very
honest with me on my percentage of the profits, and it was clear they were not
being honest at that point. We eventually settled it, but all those factors came
together, and I felt I wanted to have my own production-and-distribution
company.

SA: You'd had Film Group, though, with your brother, Gene, which
also covered production and distribution. How was the concept behind New
World different from Film Group?

RC: Film Group was a little company. I felt that it should have been a
bigger company. I folded Film Group after a year and a half or so because I
felt I didn't know enough about distribution, and the pictures were too little.
It just wasn't enough of a company. So when I started New World, I hired
Larry Woolner—who was experienced in distribution—as my sales manager
and set up a real company with our own offices. With our own staff, too—a
major production and distribution staff. It was a full break with everything
I'd done before.

SA: In your autobiography, *How I Made a Hundred Movies in Hollywood and Never Lost a Dime* (1990), you discuss the origination of the New World Pictures name, about the significance of the word "Pictures" over "Films" and "New" rather than "Free." Will you speak to that a bit?

RC: Some famous person in advertising had written a book that I had read. He said, "The two most important words for selling are 'new' and 'free.'" I thought "free" has nothing to do with the way I want to distribute films, but I can use the word "new." I put together a number of tries and ended up with New World. At first it was going to be New World Films. But I thought at the time that I didn't know that film would always be the way pictures are made and distributed. I changed the name from New World Films to New World Pictures on the basis that there would always be pictures.

SA: You'd been a producer since the start of your career practically—your earliest films *Monster from the Ocean Floor* (1954) and *The Fast and The Furious* (1955) went back many years. And you'd directed all those movies in the 1950s and 1960s. Now you were setting up yourself as something like a studio chief, a mini-mogul of sorts—is that the wrong term? You were at the top of the hierarchy.

RC: Yes, to a certain extent. I was running my own company.

SA: I get the feeling when I see the hundred or so films that came through New World—except for the ones that were simply purchased—that there's an essence there that's you. With the humor, with the action, with the bit of sex, the inclusion of a social message—that formula right there. The way the shooting was done, too. Paul Bartel around the time he was directing *Death Race 2000* said, "Roger believes, I think, in the producer as auteur. To a certain extent I think he doesn't really care that much who directs a lot of the films that he produces." We've been so conditioned by the Truffauts and that group to think that the director is the auteur of a picture, not the creative producer. What do you think?

RC: I've never even thought of the concept of the producer as the auteur. I've directed about sixty films. In general, I agree with the director as the auteur. It's just the way I work. However, having been in charge of my own company is somewhat different. Just about every film is my idea, so we start with that. I have certain ideas about the storyline, the characterizations and the themes within it. I believe that on most films the director is the auteur, but I think the statement has been carried too far. The making of motion pictures is a collaborative medium: between the producer, the director, and the writer, specifically. But also, the actors contribute. The editor contributes. The director of photography contributes.

On most films, the most important of those people will be the director; but on my own films, the ones I produce but don't direct, I have certain thoughts that I want in them. These pictures almost always start with my idea, and I will generally write a two-, three-, four-, five-page synopsis, which has the elements I want. I will work with the writer and then bring in the director on the second draft, but I want to have control of the first draft so that we're working with has my thoughts and my themes within it. Now that doesn't hold true on every picture. Very often we've had a writer-director, and the writer-director will do all of the drafts; but that's only after a full discussion with me as to what the picture will be about and what the themes will be. As I said, I work very closely with the writer, but once shooting starts I step away. I leave it totally to the director, and the director does become a semi-auteur. The director's job then, I think, primarily, is to work with the actors: to set up the shots, the compositions, the way of shooting the style, and to take charge of the editing.

So, really, the director takes charge once I have made certain that certain ideas I want are in the script. I discuss this with the director and, of course, heavily with the writer. There are a lot of producers who are there on set every day. I'm generally in there for the first one or two days, and then I almost

4

never come back to the set. I look at the dailies. I talk occasionally in the evening with the director on the phone. It works that way for us. I think one of the most successful of the writer-directors was Allan Arkush. Although he worked with Joe Dante on *Rock 'N' Roll High School*, on that one in particular I stepped back. I felt Allan knew what he wanted to do. We had discussed the picture—what was going to be in it—and I stepped back almost one-hundred percent on that.

Here is a fact few people know: more Academy Award-winning directors have started with me than, I believe, any other producer in the history of Hollywood. These are directors known as auteurs, and they got their beginning and their first training working with me. I totally respect the work of the director. I don't know where Paul got that idea about the producer as auteur. I think it's completely incorrect.

SA: Sometimes I wonder if Paul Bartel was a fairly angry guy. I don't know if it was a spiteful remark that he made about the producer potentially being the auteur. Maybe he sensed that his own individuality as a director was somewhat offset by the collaborative relationship you and he had during post on *Death Race 2000*. You notice in some of his later films where he had more control over content and style and theme that the output is not as good as when he was working with a strong producer or executive.

RC: That might be. We were pretty much in agreement with just about everything on *Death Race 2000*. Where we disagreed was in regard to the level of comedy within it. The original script was a serious script. When I came up with the idea of killing the pedestrians, I felt that we had to have humor. But this was to be humor on a serious subject. My concept was closer to a *Dr. Strangelove*-kind-of humor, and Paul's was a little bit broader. I think we worked that out fairly well because the picture was immensely successful, and it actually won a poll with the readers of *Maxim* magazine, whatever that may mean, as the greatest B picture of all time. So between us we did turn out something of some meaning.

SA: It seems to me that of the ten or eleven films Paul Bartel made what's very noticeable is that the two that are perhaps most compelling are *Private Parts* (1972) and *Death Race 2000*, which both had Cormans overseeing their creation. Gene on the first, *Private Parts*, and you on *Death Race 2000*. As I understand it, Bartel approached you at some point about *Eating Raoul* (1982).

RC: I gave him the title *Eating Raoul*. He asked me to come in on that particular picture and look at it and discuss the editing with him. His title then was *Waiting for Raoul*. I said, "Paul, the title is obviously *Eating Raoul*." I gave him a few notes on that—we got along fairly well—I thought it was a good picture.

SA: If we go back to those early years at New World, when you had people like Stephanie Rothman and Joe Viola working for you, you were looking to produce films fast. You or Julie would come up with a concept for a picture. Or maybe a Jonathan Demme would come up with a concept. And you would look to the market, anticipating what would sell. The concept would subsequently proceed to development. Then production followed, and you'd plan your roll-out with the drive-ins and theaters across the country. Right? Will you tell me about the approach to exhibition-distribution you used during these early years?

RC: We distributed in a different way at that time. Today a picture will open in two-thousand or three-thousand theaters or more. That's because you're using digital projection. With prints you can't do that because it can cost you a great deal of money—you just can't afford to buy that many prints. what we did, and what the majors were doing also, was we distributed in areas. Our plan was to buy always one-hundred prints. On each picture, we would open with those one-hundred prints in two areas, say New York and Boston. We knew that we would lose a certain number of theaters at the end of the first week. If we opened in New York or Boston, we would arrange to move, say, to Chicago and Philadelphia. Also, after the first weekend, you'd pretty much know 90 percent on most films where you stood. we would open on Friday, and if we had good grosses, we would buy another hundred prints or fifty more prints or two-hundred prints if we had a big winner. But we felt we always needed a minimum of a hundred prints. We would up that if things looked good, and then we would move those prints around to different sections of the country.

SA: How did you move them? Did you use couriers?

RC: There were motion picture distribution companies that contracted to move prints. We just worked with the normal companies that did that.

SA: How did you negotiate the bookings and screenings of the films?

RC: We had what were called franchise holders. There were a number of independent companies, and there'd be somebody, let us say, in St. Louis, who'd be an independent distributor there. He would have the franchise to distribute your films, plus three or four other companies' films in that territory. I knew who the franchise holders were around the country, and we worked with them in their individual territories. They knew the theater owners. They knew the bookers. They knew how to book their territories.

SA: Promotional material was circulated in a similar fashion?

RC: Yes.

SA: Was it Jon Davison early on who was doing the placement of the radio and TV spots?

RC: He didn't do the placement—he did the creation. Jon was the best I've ever worked with in coming up with catch lines, advertising slogans, and whole advertising campaigns—which consisted of the posters or newspaper advertising, radio spots, and TV spots

SA: When you worked up a five-page scenario or outline, you would simultaneously start to conceptualize the graphic elements for the advertising?

RC: Yes. But there's some sort of myth that we would have the poster before we made the film. Once or twice that happened—occasionally, I should say—but in general we didn't do that because we knew we would be coming up with new ideas. We would have one idea, and then we would look at the dailies and say, "Hey, here's another way to work with this."

SA: Back when New World had its offices on Sunset Boulevard, where did your technical people work? Steve Carver told me he would go home sometimes to edit, that he had a machine he borrowed from Frances Coppola. Joe Dante and Allan Arkush, on the other hand, always mention working around Jack Rabin and Associates.

RC: Jack did our special effects. We also rented editing suites at Jack Rabin's company in Hollywood. But when we built the studio, we had our own suites, back when we were still cutting on film.

SA: That was at the lumberyard studio?

RC: Yes.

SA: Can you tell me a bit about the Filipino productions? How did you decide to make films overseas like that?

RC: I had met Cirio Santiago when I took a trip around the world at the expense of American International. They wanted me to scout locations in Australia because they knew I liked to travel. They'd given me a first-class ticket. I was a young guy, and I thought, "Australia is almost half-way around the world." I called the travel bureau and said, "How much is it to change this ticket to around-the-world economy class?" I told them all the places I planned to visit. They said it would cost something like $15. So, I got a trip around the world for $15, with introductions to various filmmakers in various cities. I met Cirio on that trip and then later on John Ashley, an actor who had become a producer of low-budget films. Ashley told me about the Philippines, and so I went back and met with Cirio again because it turned out by then he was working with Ashley. I started the Philippines pictures with *The Big Doll House* (1971) with Cirio. The first picture New World had made, *The Student Nurses* (1970) was filmed in California, and it was a solid success. But *The Big Doll House* was a runaway success. One of the reasons that I kept going back to the Philippines was that it was a very interesting tropical location. Also, the cost was very low. I could get a bigger-looking picture for very little money in Manila

SA: You can't really separate Jack Hill from the Philippines productions. How did he come into your orbit?

RC: A few years earlier, before I had the distribution company—actually, when I had the Film Group—I had bought several Russian science fiction films. They were making very big, expensive science fiction pictures. Science fiction at that time, with the occasional exception, was really low-budget. I'd seen how good these were, and I bought the films. But they were filled with anti-American propaganda. I called the UCLA film department and asked them who they thought were their top graduates that year. I interviewed several people. I chose Francis Coppola—and that started his career. His first job was editing the anti-American propaganda from the Russian science fiction films. Jack had been one of the people UCLA had recommended, and I remembered him. Jack worked on various projects for me before *The Big Doll House*. He did a stock car racing picture called *Pit Stop* (1969). I thought he could handle the action and the humor of *The Big Doll House*.

9

SA: The revenues during these first couple of years were such that you would just immediately pour them into the next production, right? And New World started to expand. You had the offices in Sunset Boulevard. You were doing a lot of location footage and international shooting. What were you able to start doing once you started banking profits? How did the company's approach to production change?

RC: First, we built our own office building on San Vicente Boulevard in Brentwood. I needed bigger office space. I figured, "Why should I rent somebody else's building? I'll build my own building." And we put our own editing rooms into the new building. We needed to accommodate a bigger staff because our distribution staff as well as our production staff had grown. As I mentioned, we'd been renting editing rooms at Jack Rabin's. Now we had our own editing rooms on San Vicente.

SA: You still see in New World films made later in the 1970s, in the credits, citations for Jack Rabin and Associates. Though you'd moved on from using his editing suites, you still had him and his employees doing titles and maybe some optical work? Is that what happened?

RC: Yes. He was doing our titles, the optical work, some special effects. And we were doing some editing still at Jack Rabin's because we were making so many pictures so fast that the company grew beyond the capacity of our own editing rooms.

SA: At this point maybe you were doing between ten and fifteen pictures a year?

RC: I'd say ten to twelve. We used to call it "Feeding the Dinosaur." Having been expanded into a distribution company, we had to make enough films to keep the distribution company working at all times and pay the overhead.

SA: How long was the work day for you? For Julie? For the staff? Were you going home at night, or were you just working and working and working at the San Vicente offices?

RC: They were long days. At that time Julie had to spend most of the time with the children. We deliberately bought the building on San Vicente because we had built a house in the Pacific Palisades, and the building from our house at most was a seven- or eight-minute drive. Julie could come back and forth and sometimes brought Catherine, our first baby, to the office; so Catherine was raised a little bit at the office. As a matter of fact, on the day when Catherine was born, I remember, Julie was shooting one picture, and I was scouting locations for another. We had breakfast that morning. Then I went to scout the locations. Julie went to the set of her picture. When I came back from scouting locations, I remember people came running out of the office because we were still renting at that time. We had the penthouse. That sounds too grand—we just happened to be on the top floor area of a building on Sunset with a little space between the building and the elevator. As I came out of the elevator, people came running and said, "Julie's in the hospital giving birth to the baby." I found out later on that when she started having labor pains on the set everybody said, "You've got to get to the hospital right away." She said, "No"—and went over the production schedule for the next day before leaving to have the baby.

SA: Incredible! So tell me, please, what prompted the decision to purchase the Venice lumberyard and convert it into a studio area?

RC: Simply the fact that we were making so many pictures, and we were shooting everything on location and sometimes renting other studios for interiors. Again, just as I started renting offices and then built a building to have my own offices, I felt we were making so many films—and we were growing—that we needed a studio. We bought that old lumberyard and converted it into a studio with two soundstages. We later built a third soundstage because we were expanding so rapidly. I simply needed that space. We also put in all the editing suites, and we put in a special effects department because our first film at the studio was *Battle Beyond the Stars*, and I needed a space to build the sets. These were the most elaborate sets we'd ever had, and I needed space for a special effects department. It simply was an answer to the problem of making so many films. It now made sense to have a studio.

SA: Joe Dante and Allan Arkush explained to me that the earlier New World movies were so often shot on location in actual places and there was a fairly high cost to that—the cost of travel and getting permits to shoot, in particular. And one of the advantages of having the Venice facility was you could do more of everything in-house.

RC: That's a correct statement. But we still shot heavily on location. I'm a strong believer in shooting on actual locations whenever possible because you get a better sense of realism. Yet at the same time there is a cost factor in travelling to the locations. Even when we were shooting primarily at the studio, we were still shooting with a fair amount of location work simply because I liked the realism.

SA: How do you think the movies changed when you set up shop in Venice? The sets are sort of contained. There's almost a claustrophobic effect, which is very complementary when you have a movie like *Galaxy of Terror*. It adds compression and amplifies the suspense. You no longer have the openness in that picture, say, that you have in *Angels Hard as They Come* (1971) or *Grand Theft Auto* (1977).

RC: Actually, I'm not certain in retrospect that the studio added any particular quality to the pictures other than in pictures like *Battle Beyond the Stars* and a number of other science fiction pictures we were making, some of the pictures that required more-or-less-elaborate-for-our-budgets sets to be built. I still like the idea of shooting on location as much as possible. I'm not certain we added any particular quality by shooting in the studio. As a matter of fact, I think we lost a little bit of the sense of openness and the realism of shooting on location. That is one of the reasons I eventually sold the studio. I sold the studio for three reasons ultimately. I was not convinced that shooting that much on sets was adding to the pictures except for certain pictures, when we needed the studio work. Also, we had picked the location for real estate value, where we thought the real estate would go up. And we were starting to make fewer films when I sold the studio. I didn't really need that much space anymore.

SA: You were making fewer films in the early 1980s because budgets were going up?

RC: We were making fewer film because back when we started every film got a full theatrical release. I actually don't remember the year we sold the studio, but we were starting to lose theatrical distribution. This is one of the major changes for low-budget and medium-budget shooting over the years. For the first twenty or thirty years that I made films, every film got a full theatrical release. This loss started in the 1990s and then accelerated through the years, where the major studios were releasing pictures in a greater number of theaters and were beginning to dominate theatrical distribution. You're in a situation now where almost every picture in large theatrical release is a major studio—or at least a more expensive—film; and only occasionally does a low-budget film get a full theatrical release. It still happens, but it's been cut down, and we eventually sold the studio and closed our theatrical distribution department for that reason.

SA: You sold New World in 1983. Did you sell the property in Venice at the same time?

RC: When I sold New World all I sold was the name "New World" and our distribution arm. Three motion picture lawyers, Harry E. Sloan, Larry

Kupin and Larry A. Thompson, had done some dealing with us and realized how profitable all of this was, and they wanted to get into the business. Our name had become somewhat powerful. We used to say we were the strongest independent distribution company in America. We might have been right. Both Bob Shaye at New Line and the Weinstein brothers when they started said they were aware of what I had done at New World. The lawyers were really wanting the New World name and our distribution arm. What they didn't understand was that I was able to put together another distribution company very quickly because I knew all the players, as it were. It was not really that difficult to sell the distribution company and start a new one.

SA: The day after you sold New World you started the next company, Concorde Pictures, right?

RC: Yes. I moved across the street, and I rented a building because everything was set up there. I simply moved into a building with smaller offices and operated out of that for a year, and during that year I was distributing through New World, my old distribution company. So then after a year, they bought a building, and I moved back in to the San Vincente location and started my new distribution company.

SA: My knowledge is a bit shaky here. Did the group that bought New World also purchase the Venice facility?

RC: No. That was sold ultimately to a real estate developer.

SA: You wanted to somewhat narrow your operation, and that was the impetus for selling New World and also to pull back a bit from distribution?

RC: No. I sold New World simply because Sloan, Kupin and Thompson offered me more money than I thought the name was worth. I sold them the name and the distribution company. I knew I could start another distribution

14

company very easily, so for me all I was doing was selling the name "New World." And they offered me a great money to do so, so it had no real impact on my operations.

SA: Somehow it was in my head that distribution had become somewhat messy, and there was a thrust to go back to a simpler model. Was there any sadness as you gave up the New World name?

RC: No.

SA: Let's talk about your story editors, Frances Doel in particular. She worked with you for several years. How did you wind up hiring her?

RC: Before I started New World, I was working in England. I was doing the last of the Poe pictures, *The Tomb of Ligeia* (1964). I had done some graduate work at Oxford, and I knew how good their English literature department was. I called Oxford and said I was looking for somebody as a story editor; they sent a number of people that I interviewed. I thought Frances was the brightest, and she came over and worked with me for a couple years before I started New World and then stayed at New World. She left with Barbara Boyle when Barbara went to Orion, but then she didn't really like being at Orion, and she came back to us and stayed until she finally retired. Frances was really brilliant as a story editor.

SA: Tell me a bit about the process of story development. You would study the trades, chat with your marketing people, Larry Woolner, that sort of thing, and you'd get a concept—nurses, teachers, or bikers or whatever. Then you'd work out your five-page outline. Would you then give that to Frances or a particular writer if you had one in mind? Or you would pass it on to a director? How did that work?

RC: I'd be discussing the ideas from the beginning with Frances so that

15

she was in on the inception of each picture and would be working with me on the original ideas and then continue working with the writer through development of the script and to a certain extent with the directors. Directors would always come in with certain ideas, and she would say to them: "All right we can use this idea. But this idea, we think, is not right."

SA: How did the company's signature formula of blending humor, action, sex and social message come about?

RC: That was really my thought. These were the elements I thought would be commercially successful and also would satisfy my desire to make films that were a little bit more than commercially successful, that I would consider to be good pictures even though they were made on a low-budget cost.

SA: I'm wondering because *The Intruder*, which you'd directed long before you created New World, is a wonderful film. But you've indicated elsewhere that maybe it was too direct with its rhetoric. In subsequent movies you directed and produced, you often would blend the social message with elements that are more commercial, such as the sex, the humor, and the action. I guess what I'm getting at is your impulse toward social justice persisted throughout those thirteen years or so at New World, but a lot of people don't recognize this tendency because the films you made during these years are so outwardly commercial.

RC: What you're saying is correct. What happened was this: *The Intruder* got wonderful reviews. I still remember the first line from a review in one of the New York newspapers: "*The Intruder* is a major credit to the entire American film industry." But though the reviews were brilliant, the film failed commercially. Eventually we got our money back with the DVDs thirty years later, but at the time the film was a failure. I felt I was too overt in my theme, or my messages, as it were. I'd forgotten, or ignored, on that film that a film

16

must have entertainment value. I learned from *The Intruder* that I still had these certain progressive ideas and themes I wanted in the pictures. If you're familiar with method acting, there's the text and the subtext: the text is what is said and the subtext is the meaning behind what is said. I thought, "From here on in the themes will be the subtext." That is, in the action pictures, in the humor, in the R-rated commercially-oriented films, there will be themes beneath that are important to me. But they always will be subordinate to the entertainment value so the audience gets the entertainment that the titles indicate and the advertisements say. The theme is an added bonus. In some cases, I would assume, a large portion of the audience wouldn't even get the theme because it was sublimated to such an extent, but it was in there—really to satisfy me. It was something I wanted.

SA: You know, with *The Intruder* you have this handsome, young Bill Shatner, who comes into a southern town, and he has this hateful rhetoric and works up disaffected white people. I was thinking that what's so remarkable, and this is an instance of life imitating art, is that you have this public figure now, Richard Spencer, who is a handsome-ish, leading man-looking guy who's set himself up as a leader of the alt-right with his crypto-Nazi talk. There's a remarkable doubling between Shatner in *The Intruder* and Spencer in real life. Any thoughts on that?

RC: Yes. I think that type of character has been with America forever and probably will be for the foreseeable future. What was going on to a certain extent in the 1960s is going on again today.

SA: The opportunities and support you've given to women can't be overlooked. New World provided early work opportunities to Stephanie Rothman, Gale Anne Hurd, Amy Jones, Penelope Spheeris, Barbara Peeters, Jane Rhum, Tina Hirsch. Barbara Boyle served as a vice president at the company while Julie was a producer. You were always ready to buck the system, the "man's game," if you will. Why?

17

RC: It wasn't so much that I was looking to give women a start. It was that I wanted the best possible person for each individual position. And the situation was that most people in the American entertainment industry were picking men for these positions. Therefore the pool of available people included more women than men because of the proclivity of others to pick men. What I was doing was I was simply saying I want the best person irrespective of their sex. In many cases the woman was simply the superior person. We ended up with more women—executives, writers, directors, producers, and so forth—because I wanted the best person, and very often that person was a woman.

SA: But there is a noticeable streak in the New World movies and later in the Concorde films and earlier with the AIP movies that you didn't have a problem with women being depicted as strong sorts of figures. They are sex kittens, often, but they are also radicals and individuals and political bomb throwers in some instances. Is this tendency in many of the movies an instance of that radical political outlook you had started to explore as a director in the 1950s?

RC: Yes. I've always been on the radical end of politics and of culture. Very often that has led me to women. With the discrimination against women, the radical component of my thinking has led me to empower women. It's part of a movement against the establishment.

SA: This tendency crossed over into progressive depictions of minorities in the films, as well, and also led to numerous work opportunities for minorities.

RC: Yes. We were featuring a number of black actors and actresses. Pam Grier, who became really quite a star in several pictures made in the 1970s and '80s, started with us.

SA: You were a mentor to Carl Franklin, too. But that was after New World, I guess.

RC: Yes. Carl Franklin did several pictures for us.

SA: What do you think, looking back, were the best pictures made during the New World-era of your career? Which ones really pop out in your memory as being the best?

RC: *Death Race 2000*, as I said, won a poll as the greatest B picture of all time, so I have to put that in. I then would put in *Piranha*, *Rock 'N' Roll High School*, *Jackson County Jail*, *Grand Theft Auto*, *Big Bad Mama* (1974).

SA: Any of the pictures Jonathan Demme directed?

RC: Yes. Jonathan did *Crazy Mama* (1975), a follow-up to *Big Bad Mama*. I would include that, too.

SA: What do you think of *Caged Heat* (1974)?

RC: *Caged Heat*—I would put that in close, but I would still put *Crazy Mama* ahead of *Caged Heat*.

SA: Would you speak to the disappointments, the pictures that lack a certain quality or panache, or the ones that stumbled at the box office?

RC: I've probably blocked most disappointments out. I can't really think of anything.

SA: What about something like *Cockfighter* (1974)?

RC: Yes. You're absolutely right. As I said, I forget the disappointments.

Cockfighter was a very good novel by Charles Willeford, and I thought, "There's never been a picture about cockfighting. This is a chance to do something that's never been done before." The picture was directed by Monte Hellman. It was a good picture. But I found out why there'd never been a picture about cockfighting: people didn't want to see a picture about cockfighting. I completely forgot it. You're right to bring that up.

SA: Why do you think pictures like *Jackson County Jail* and *Piranha*—ones you just named—and others like *The Velvet Vampire* (1971), *Night Call Nurses* and *The Slumber Party Massacre* (1982)—still resonate with contemporary audiences?

RC: I would say we understood that these were genres films, and we understood the conventions of the genre films and followed them. But we tried to offer more so that the audience got to see the entertainment value of the film they expected to see based on the title and the advertising. And then we gave them a little bit more. For instance, in *Death Race 2000* and *Jackson County Jail*, there were clear overtones in which we commented on the politics and culture of the day. Even *Piranha*, to a slightly lesser extent, said something about capitalist society and the military role in the society. *Grand Theft Auto* was made in the 1970s when the power of television to intrude into people's lives was becoming evident; it was obviously a car-chase action comedy, but there was a little comment within that.

SA: Several film people you've mentored—Jonathan Demme and Ron Howard, for example—in interviews over the years have mentioned a talk that you often give to directors that's basically a film school education compressed into an hour and a half, or a film school education compressed into twenty minutes or ten minutes or even five minutes. Would you share some of those techniques and strategies you pass on to your new directors about making movies?

RC: I start with an understanding of how much the first-time director already knows. Has he or she gone to film school? Has he been an editor? A writer? A second unit director? And so forth. Then I try to add something. For instance, film school graduates, in particular, know a great deal of theory of film, so there's no point going in to that. I try not to repeat what people already know. Instead I try to tell them things I've learned as a director myself, from experience. The first thing I give them is a talk about the importance of pre-production planning. Our normal schedule is generally a fifteen-day schedule, which is fairly fast. I explain they should not come in to the shooting expecting to make major decisions on the set. The major decisions should be made before so that most of the time on the set is actually done shooting, since the key concepts have been made. I'm a believer in sketching your shots in advance. Some directors like to go ahead and improvise on the set. I recognize that theory, but I don't believe in it.

There are other directors, say a Jean-Luc Godard—I'm speaking of those days when he was famous for improvising on the set. The opposite would be Hitchcock, who would have every single shot sketched and would shoot exactly according to what he had sketched. I would be somewhere in the middle but a little bit closer to Hitchcock. I would say, "I want you to sketch all of your shots." Now I know from experience that hardly anybody ever really does that; but if they can sketch 70 or 80 or 90 percent of their shots, they have enough to work with. But then I say, "You must always be flexible. You take your preparation—that is the basis of the way you work—but you should be free to improvise a little bit around that. You get a better idea on the set and you change it. If something you plan doesn't work out, then you've got to substitute in some way." I emphasize that to a great deal.

The same thing with actors. I usually talk to the actors in order to "work out," as we say in method terminology, the motivations and the characterizations. If possible, rehearse a little bit. But you can't rehearse too much because of Screen Actors Guild rules as to how much you have to pay the actors and so forth but enough rehearsal, in short, to get the basic outlines of the character set so that the director and the actor are in agreement. The discussions on the set with the actor should be mainly about little refinements so that, essentially, you spend your time shooting the picture, not deciding what to shoot.

I give directors certain practical things, too. For instance: "Try to arrange your shooting so you've broken down the scene. You know that a certain number of shots are going to be in one direction and another in another direction. Try to do all of your shots in one direction, one after another, so you're not jumping back and forth." As you know, I've had more Academy Award-winning directors, I believe, start with me than anybody else. But there are some directors who have not gone on. There was one director, I remember, on the first day of shooting.... We were shooting a night scene. Now, normally, we do not start with a night scene, but for whatever reason we had to start with a night scene, and we were shooting in a vacant lot between two buildings. The director said, "All right, the first shot is in this direction to building A." And they got the shot. Then the director said, "Now we're reversing, and we are at the one-hundred-and-eighty degree move, and we're shooting the reverse of that shot on the other person on building B." They tore down all the lighting and put up all the lighting for building B. After that, he said, "Now we go back, and we shoot a different shot, but it's in the same direction as building A." So they had to tear down all the lighting and go back and put up all the lighting that they'd first put up for the first shot. The gaffer, the head electrician, got in his car and left. "I don't need to work with an idiot," he said. "I'll get another job in a couple of days someplace else."

In other words, this director did not understand that it was taking an hour to change the lighting. He should have been shooting, as I tell them, "as much as you can to keep all your shots in one direction to save on the lighting." Sometimes you're tempted to just go right in and shoot. But in order to do that, you must rehearse the scene fully because your shooting out of sequence, and the actors must understand the entire blocking of the scene so that they'll be able to adjust to shooting out of sequence. These are simply practical things you're not really taught in film school. When he was planning

Boxcar Bertha (1972), Marty Scorsese sketched every single shot; he was the most conscientious about shooting every single shot.

On preparation for *Grand Theft Auto*, I remember telling Ron Howard: "You can't come in the first day and say, 'Where will I put the camera?' You've got to know where you put the camera." I still remember this because Ron had never directed; he'd been an actor. A crew sort of sizes up a director to see, as we say, "Did he do his homework, and where do we stand?" I remember we were shooting the opening scene—it was in a house in Brentwood—and Ron came in. Everybody's looking to see this actor as a director. What will he do? He came in, and I remember this almost exactly word for word. He said, "The actress comes in that door there, walks over to the sofa, and sits down. Then she picks up a telephone. The camera will be on a dolly here." He pointed to this spot with a thirty lens. "We will dolly with the actress and pan with the actress to point B. When she sits down and picks up the phone, we cut at that point, and we will cut to a close-up of her picking up the phone."

The crew knew immediately that Ron had prepared. He knew exactly what the first shot was going to be. I always thought he had rehearsed that in his mind after what I'd told him, so that he would come in and say exactly what he wanted, including which lens he wanted on the camera on the first shot.

BARBARA BOYLE

Interview by Stephen B. Armstrong

STEPHEN B. ARMSTRONG: How did you and Roger Corman become acquainted?

BARBARA BOYLE: Roger and I first crossed paths when he made a series of movies for American International Pictures. I was a lawyer. When I graduated from UCLA Law School, the person who gave me my very first job was a man named Sam Arkoff. He was an extraordinary man. He was one of the owners of American International before it went public, he and Jim Nicholson. The strangeness of being a young woman at twenty-five—before there were pantsuits, when you wore really short skirts and really high heels being a professional woman—surprised people. Sam had some of the best lines I ever heard. In those days, someone would come in for a meeting and say, "But you're a girl!" Then they would ask questions like "Did you really go to law school? Did you graduate? Did you take the bar?" Another frequent question was "Can I see Sam?" I would answer, "If he's available, of course." I would take them to Sam's office and say, "I should leave you alone." And Sam would say, 'No. No. What's the problem?" They'd say, "You know, Sam, she's a girl." And Sam would respond, "Oh, I never noticed." I thought that was just a great answer.

The account that I handled at AIP was the Corman films, which at that time were the horror movies. Edgar Allan Poe's writings had come into public domain, and Roger and AIP had the idea to make a series of films based upon Poe's stories. I was on the other side of the desk from Roger and his attorney. He, too, back in the early-sixties was very, very—I won't say awestruck—but he found it interesting that I was a woman, and a lawyer, and had the academic credentials that I did. Roger liked me. He and my husband and I became friends. In 1965, I had my first child, and Roger, who was not then married, came over. I had been working for AIP in New York for the past three years. Roger came to see my baby, and it was like: "Oh, yeah, that's the baby." Then he said, "Since you've been in New York, AIP hasn't done any of my formal contracts." I said, "Too bad." And he went on, "I have an idea." "Well, what is it?" He answered, "Represent me." I said, "I drafted those contracts." "I know," he said, "and wouldn't it be fun to negotiate against Sam."

That began my work as Roger's lawyer. I guess it was 1966 or 1967 or 1968, somewhere in there. In 1968, I started a law firm with a fellow UCLA Law graduate. Corman retained the law firm to do all his work. He paid us a retainer of $100 thousand a year, which, in 1968, was a lot of money. I did all the production work for Roger's movies and for the films he did for major studios like *Von Richthofen and Brown*. Whatever he did—except for taxes and estate planning—that was movie-related, I negotiated and drafted the contract. We established two companies, New World Productions and New World Pictures. In 1969 or '70, we had the first film, an exploitation film. It was a tremendous box office success, and Roger started badgering me in 1970. "I pay you so much money. Why don't you come and work for me, and you won't have to share it with your partner? Come work for me. We're getting very busy. I don't know what to do about U.S. distribution. Come and work for me." Finally, in 1972, I went to work for Roger.

SA: That first film was Stephanie Rothman's *The Student Nurses*?

BB: Could have been. Or *The Student Teachers* (1970). We had already done *Boxcar Bertha,* which is how I met Marty Scorsese at AIP in 1968. Marty had had said to Roger, "I'm trying to put together this movie, *Mean Streets* (1973), and I need a lawyer. You've been successful. Whoever he is, I want him to represent me in Los Angeles." Corman said, "It is not a he, it's a she, but you should meet her." That's how I came to represent Scorsese from *Mean Streets* to *Alice Doesn't Live Here Anymore* (1974). I did all the production work for *Mean Streets.* I set up the distribution deal. It wasn't very financially successful, but it was a launch for Harvey's career, Marty's career and Bobby's career. The next picture that Marty did was a "big studio picture" called *Alice Doesn't Live Here Anymore.* By that time, real money was involved for Marty as a director. Then right after, I went to work for Roger around 1972. That's the best I can remember.

In the tradition of Corman, one after another young filmmakers came to the only school in the 1970s for film: Corman. He had studied at Stanford, and Gale Anne Hurd, also a Stanford graduate, came to Los Angeles to become his assistant. She is very gracious in giving credit to me. I was married with children and working full-time, and a lawyer. I gave her the possibility that women could do it all. Jim Cameron was in the arts department making miniatures. There were all these incredible film artists.

Everybody was afraid of Roger, except me. Everyone came and talked to me to get Roger to do whatever they wanted. There was a real run from NYU after Scorsese: Demme and Davison; Joe Dante showed up, too. The Ds were prominent for a few years. As I say, everyone was afraid of Roger, and no one was afraid of me. I heard all the stories and everything else.

I began to make an analysis about distribution and determined that the real money was in distribution. I had the idea of starting what were then offices across the country. The country was divided by the major studios into thirteen territories. There were the Western states, there were the Mountain states, there were the Eastern states. They were in clusters. I opened a series of what were called "exchanges." That was really an incredible move in those ten years before there was a profusion of independent distributors. AIP went public and became Filmways, and to Sam Arkoff's dying breath he was sorry about that. Even through a time of raising a lot of cash from Wall Street, Corman never wanted to do it. I wanted to do it because I wanted others in the company to benefit, but he never wanted to. He was very happy to control production and very happy to have his own distribution network in the domestic marketplace. We made a lot of money, I must say. It was very successful.

I had one major problem. From October to May, I couldn't collect from the exhibitors. I couldn't collect money, that is, because I had no product to give them. We were making summer product and drive-in product with *Women in Cages* (1971), *Night of the Cobra Woman* (1972) and *The Student Nurses*. Ron Howard had one with *Grand Theft Auto*. There were multiple pictures by these directors until their budgets went up, at which point Roger would wish them well and send them onto the next level. The reason for the women directors, and Roger himself will tell you, was because "They are more loyal, they are smarter and they are cheaper.

SA: Was he, in that sense, exploiting them?

BB: I don't think so at all. He gave women who wouldn't have really had a shot—from Alex Rose to Gale Anne Hurd—incredible opportunities at a level they wouldn't have had otherwise. Gale was his assistant for four short months, and afterwards she was an associate producer; then she was a producer. Roger's idea was that if you gave somebody a chore, or gave them a task to do and they did it, and they did it very well, then give them the task just above that. They go right up the ladder. That's what he did. When they were to a point where they were really valuable outside of the New World universe, he would wish them well. He'd say, "My God, somebody's going to give you $1.2 million to do that movie? That's wonderful. Keep in touch." He would've given them the same $400 thousand he'd always been giving them. If Embassy or United Artists or somebody else offered to do it for more money, he thought that was great. There were plenty of people who stayed with New World all their lives. But for those who had the ability, the desire and the discipline, there was no training school like New World.

That's why for women I don't think it was exploitation. I guess you can call anything in this particular #MeToo climate "exploitation" or "sexual exploitation" because we're getting very, very—and rightly so—sensitive to the gender gaps in our own industry that have always been there and maybe always will be there. But in terms of a first start, how do you graduate from Stanford, not even majoring in film, and get a job as Roger Corman's assistant a week after you graduate? Nowhere in the Hollywood that existed then. In the late 1960s and early 1970s, you might have gotten a job—if you were a guy—in the mailroom. Roger created an incredibly encouraging environment. He truly didn't see the difference between men and women. There were men directors, and there were women directors: for him it was just all about the talent.

I'll finish up with the idea of the exchanges. There I was, pondering how to collect the money exhibitors owe us from the summer releases when I have no new product from October through March. Paul Kohner, a brilliant agent for many international directors, called me and said, "I'd like you to take a look at Ingmar Bergman's new movie, *Cries & Whispers*. I thought it would be good if Roger released this prestigious movie." I said, "Well, how much do you want as an advance?" He said, "$75 thousand." I said, "Let me think about this."

I thought to myself, "Roger loves Ingmar Bergman. He's one of the directors Roger admires. Now the question is: 'How do I get $75 thousand? Because Roger won't put it up.'" I called Films Inc., which was a non-theatrical distributor in those days, based in Illinois. They had acquired a bunch of our exploitation movies for shut-ins, hospitals, planes and all kinds of non-theatrical venues. I asked the head of Films, Inc. what he thought of *Cries & Whispers* and Bergman. He said, "We don't really deal with foreign language films very much, but I love Bergman and I'd love to do it." I told him how much we wanted as an advance, and he agreed.

Then I went to Roger and told him that Paul Kohner called and he wanted New World to acquire *Cries & Whispers* for U.S. and Canadian distribution, for a $75 thousand advance. But I had negotiated that amount from Films, Inc. for the non-theatrical rights. It may be an answer to my issue of how to collect because this is a film that would be played in the fall. At that time, the guys who owned the drive-ins also began to own the chains that were evolving. Roger said he loved the whole deal. The film ended up being artistically and commercially extremely successful. Our investment was one print in New York. One print at that time, we're talking about $40 thousand. Roger said to me afterward, "Go and do it again." And that's how I managed to acquire twenty-five of the greatest movies in the world in the ten years I was there. Not only were they films that I liked, and that Roger loved, but they filled the spot from October to March, which allowed me to collect for our summer pictures.

I often traveled to acquire foreign language films as Roger did not want to go on any buying trips. I would not only select the films that coincided with his taste, but I would then make the best possible deal. I went to Cannes, New York and London. I picked up *The Story of Adele H* (1975), and then I had the next three Truffaut movies. I had acquired *The Lost Honour of Katherina Blum* (1975). I picked up *Amarcord* (1973) from a screening. I was in Cannes most frequently with Frank Moreno, who is absolutely brilliant. He was with me through many of those years as the head of marketing and distribution as we now know it. At the time, he did everything, from booking theatres to buying movies. He had the best eye for finished films than anyone I've ever met, whether you're talking about *The Harder They Come* (1972) or *Small Change* (1976).

But the best acquisition story I have from that period is *The Tin Drum* (1979). As I said, I had acquired at the New York Film Festival a film called *The Lost Honour of Katharina Blum*, which Volker Schlöndorff directed. The film had not been very financially successful, but I had Films, Inc. backing me with any kind of money I had to advance. Among the non-English language films I had acquired and even a couple of the English-language films—*The Harder They Come* and *The Kids Are Alright* (1979), a couple like that—we had done really well through our exchanges and through playing them.

Frank and I were, as usual, in Cannes. Frank was there for the whole period, but I was there for one week only to make the deals and look at anything Frank had looked at.

Cannes is a beautiful place that's overrun by all the people you want to avoid when you're in L.A., as far as I'm concerned. We saw *Mon oncle d'Amerique* (1980), a Resnais film, and acquired it. Frank told me I needed to see *The Tin Drum*, which had been directed by Volker Schlöndorff. I told him I'd read the book and loved it, but I didn't want Volker or anyone to stay an extra day because I was going to Paris to see Truffaut and all the plans were already made. I told Frank that if he liked it, I would make a deal without seeing it before I left. Frank told me the production cost millions, but he thought we would be looking at $400 thousand as an advance. I said, "The question is: are we going to gross enough?" The thinking was straightforward: we are paying an advance against the producer's share of revenue from distribution. We charge interest on the advance, and so long as we're sure we're going to recoup that money, we are fine. Remember, it was pretty much a theatrical market only. Frank's answer, "Yes," was enough for me.

I met with the producer of the film the day before I was leaving. I told him, "Schlöndorff's a wonderful director, and Frank has seen the movie. I am ready to make a deal with you." He said, "What are you going to offer?" I said, "I understand it's going to cost us a lot of money. What are you looking for?" He said that he was looking for $400 thousand. I said, "How about $300 thousand as an advance against your share and some really good terms on the back end?" I told him it didn't matter what the movie cost—it matters what people were willing to pay for it. And there was little to no competition then for foreign language films.

He said to me, "Can we meet tomorrow?" I told him I was leaving Cannes at noon, but we could certainly have a coffee. We met the next morning, and he said, "I've given this careful consideration, and I'm not asking for

$400 thousand; I'm asking for $500 thousand." I looked at him and said, "Thank you so much for meeting with me and coming this morning. I have to catch my plane." And he said, shaking my hand, "Oh, *madame*, why?" I told him, "Yesterday, you'd asked for $400 thousand, and I'd thought we'd meet somewhere in the middle." He said that he'd heard I was a really, really tough negotiator, and if I had offered $300 thousand, it must have been worth $500 thousand. I said, "This is the kind of negotiator I am. Tough or not, when I make an offer, it's going to be somewhere in the vicinity of where I end up. Your job is to find out where I end up. You don't change your request on me." I got my luggage and walked away.

When I came back, Roger said, "You got Resnais's film. I'm so happy. What happened with *The Tin Drum*?" I told him the story, and Roger said, "Good for you. What did Frank think it would make?" I told him, "Frank said it would make about $500 thousand producer's share, so I was willing to go to $400 thousand. But something with a $500 thousand advance, which requires $2 million box office, was too close to comfort for me. It isn't like Films, Inc. is going to give me this kind of an advance; they're going to give me $75 thousand-$100 thousand. So we're really on the limb."

Months passed. It was not the time of emails and rapid information flow. I lost track of *The Tin Drum*. Roger had fourteen deals in various stages of production. There was just so much to do. Three or four months later my assistant, over the intercom, says, "There's a man on the phone. He's got an accent. His name is Volker Schlöndorff. Do you know who that is?" I said, "I do. Put him on." He got on the phone and said, "Mrs. Boyle, I know you wanted to acquire *The Tin Drum*, and I know you regarded my film *The Lost Honour of Katharina Blume* as not so financially successful for you. I'm sorry the deal did not work out." I said, "The real mistake, in my business, is acquiring films that are unsuccessful; I must try to insure against risk. I hope *The Tin Drum* goes out and earns a lot of revenue." He told me that it had never gotten U.S. distribution. He asked me to see the film. I told him, "It doesn't matter what I think of the film. I'm not here to fall in love with a film. I have an obligation to my company and to Roger." Volker said, "I just want you to see it."

I'm a very frank person, and I think all films are a miracle when they get made. But I loved *The Tin Drum*, and I thought it was brilliant. I told him that I wouldn't work with that producer. Their agent at that time was Paul Kohner, I think, whom I knew well. I told him that we could cut to the quick, and I would give them $400 thousand, which is what the guy asked me for, which was far more generous than I needed to be. We made the deal. It went on to win an Academy Award. It made a pile of money. It's a brilliant film.

Those were the kinds of deals we did. You can say how brilliant I was to want to bring these international films to America because I liked them so much. But the initial motivation for me was that I needed to collect money from October to March and having deliverable films for exhibition during that period was the way. It was very calculated. The first one and the second one worked. They were very successful. Roger put his name on them, and we went to the Academy Awards more than once. It was a wonderful time.

Now let me tell you a Ron Howard story. Ron had made one film for us that he acted in, *Eat My Dust!* Roger paid him half-a-million dollars; I remember this very well. It was more than any picture had cost, and it was more than he'd ever paid anybody since New World Pictures and New World Productions were formed. The picture was wildly successful. Roger wanted to do a sequel, and he wanted me to talk to Ron. Ron and I met, and he said, "I want to direct the next one." I told him, "You would have to star in it, for sure. Roger will pay you no more money than your actor fee. You'll have to write the script for next to nothing, and you'll have to direct for next to nothing." He told me that he had made a film at USC. I said, "Okay, go and see Roger. Tell him you'll do the next picture for the same amount of money that you got for the first one. You won't up your price, and you'll star in it, and you will write it for next to nothing, but you want to direct it. And Roger will say, 'Have you ever made a film before?' And you'll show him your short." I added, "Roger will want Jon Davison to produce and Joe Dante to direct second unit". Ron was fine with that, and it meant we knew it would be on time, and we knew Dante would be there because he'd already directed a picture for Roger.

After Ron's meeting with Roger, Roger came to my office to tell me he had closed the deal with Ron Howard: Ron was to star in the follow-up, *Grand Theft Auto*, Ron Howard and Rance Howard would write, and Ron wanted to direct it. Roger told me that Ron had directed a short film and it was good. Finally, Roger added he was giving him Joe Dante for a second unit director, and Jon Davison to produce.

The person who recently reminded me of this story was Ron Howard himself. That's the way it worked with Roger. Roger loved Ron, loved the two movies, and they made a fortune and a directing career for Ron.

SA: *Grand Theft Auto* is a really good film, too.

BB: Yes, they're all good films.

JACK HILL

Interview by Robert Powell

ROBERT POWELL: *Blood Bath* (1966), *Ich Ein Groupie* (1970) and *Sorceress* (1982) were three Roger Corman films that you contributed to significantly as a director but for which you did not receive sole credit. What did you learn from working on these films?

JACK HILL: Some of the scenes I directed in *Track of the Vampire* (1966) I showed to another producer, who wanted to do a picture with me. When I submitted *Spider Baby* (1967) to people who wanted to finance it, I showed scenes to them from my film *Blood Bath*. The picture was not complete, but I had shot a lot of stuff and showed the scenes to these people, showing them I knew how to direct. It was one of those Roger Corman things where he bought a Yugoslavian movie with a lot of good material in it that was supposed to be a horror movie. When we looked at it, it was not a horror movie at all; it was kind of a crime thriller, a murder mystery. And my job was to pull out whatever footage I could use to make a horror movie. I wrote and directed whole new scenes so that I could incorporate some of the scenes from the Yugoslavian movie.

Because the look of the footage was so different, Roger Corman decided to release the original film, which was called *Operation: Titian* (1963) as best he could and use the footage that I shot. He got Stephanie Rothman to take

35

the footage that I shot and write and direct more to make a complete story out of it. She turned it into a vampire movie called *Blood Bath,* and she ruined it. I wrote it as a suspense-thriller-horror movie. I thought it was a mess. It now seems to be of great historical interest. The British company Arrow Films released the movie on DVD and Blu-ray and did a whole production on it, which left me thinking, "Who in the world would ever want to see such a thing?"

Ich Ein Groupie is the one I went off to Switzerland to do with Erwin C. Dietrich. They said they would send me the script for *Ich Ein Groupie.* I was getting worried because you normally have a script more than a week or two before shooting. I got off the plane in Switzerland, and they did not have a script or story. All they had was a title. Needless to say, I tried my best to make it; I wanted a challenge. Ultimately it got to the point that the producer, Dietrich, was so impossible to deal with I couldn't do it. He finished the picture himself. When I saw the final finished picture, two thirds of it was mine, and I never got a dime out of it. Dietrich advertised the picture as a Roger Corman production. Roger learned about Dietrich advertising the picture using his name. Dietrich's company was in a small European tax haven country, and he could not be sued. We got a lawyer, and ultimately we got the guy on criminal charges. When Roger originally wrote to him about using his name and that he should get the picture, the guy wrote back and said that he was not using Roger's name. Roger's name was on the envelope in which the guy sent us the letter. Roger was paid big time on this, and I never made a dime from it.

RP: This same type of encroachment was threatened during the genesis of *The Big Doll House.* According to Calum Waddell, the original script for the film was thrown out and Stephanie Rothman, the director of Corman's *The Student Nurses,* was reportedly seeking to take over the film. Corman may have wanted to hand the directing of *The Big Doll House* over to her. How did you overcome these obstacles to make a film that practically began an entirely new film genre?

JH: This is connected to *Ich Ein Groupie*. Roger wanted to do a women-in-prison film. I knew a writer who had something, and I thought it was a pretty good script. *The Big Doll House* was the title. I had this deal to go to Switzerland to direct *Ich Ein Groupie*. I went off to Switzerland, and the idea was that as soon as I got back from that job, I was to start working on *The Big Doll House*. In the meantime, Stephanie Rothman had taken over the project, not as director, but as scriptwriter. She got another writer of her own to write a whole new script to be set in the Philippines, which I thought was insane because it was supposed to be an American type of story in an American prison. My deal with Roger was that I was going to direct this picture. And his attorney agreed, so he had to hand it to me. I took the script, which I thought was awful, and rewrote most of it on the job during the shooting. It turned out to be a huge, huge hit.

RP: After shooting *The Big Doll House*, what were your main thoughts and feelings about it?

JH: I never saw any of the footage until I returned to America. The main thing I tried to do was put a lot of humor into it that was not there before. The humor in it was the main thing that created an audience for it. It was very funny in places.

RP: Corman initially felt that *The Big Doll House* was too sexy, rough and raw. Did you then, or do you now, agree with that assessment?

JH: He was a little nervous about it because it was pretty extreme, like some of my films are. Once he showed it to his distributors, they all felt that they had a big hit on their hands. Boy, by today's standards, it is not too sexy, rough or raw at all. Maybe it was a little ahead of its time.

RP: Did the success of *The Big Doll House* fall short of, meet or exceed your expectations?

JH: It exceeded everybody's expectations. It was important because it put me on the map. I had a meeting with the head of production at MGM because of the box office numbers it was getting. Roger made a fortune on it and was kind enough to let me have my percentage. What could be more important than having a bit hit?

RP: You told Calum Waddell that *The Big Doll House* was not something that you really wanted to do? Why?

JH: I wanted to do the film with the original script that I got from a very good writer and submitted. But what happened in the meantime was that Roger made a deal with these guys in the Philippines. They told him how much they could make the picture for by shooting it in the Philippines. The cost of making a movie in the Philippines was so low, but it required a completely different script. My heart sank, and I said, "Oh, my God, what am I going to do with this?" Once receiving the new script, I was appalled at some of it because it was so bananas. I took it as a challenge. I felt that I could rewrite it, make it interesting, make it funny and do a lot of things with it. I changed my mind. I thought that it could be a lot of fun. It could be a big hit. When they reviewed it, they were very excited about it. They thought they had a winner. As it turned out, it was.

RP: How did you manage to be given the nod for writing honors in *The Big Bird Cage* (1982)?

JH: Roger wanted to do a sequel, another film in the Philippines. So I said okay and did the best I could. The success of the first film is the only reason I was given writing honors for *The Big Bird Cage*. When you've got a hit picture, you want to come out with a sequel right away. That is what you do.

38

RP: *The Big Bird Cage* includes less female nudity and torture than *The Big Doll House*. Were you given any instructions by Corman *not* to exceed the sex and violence of *The Big Doll House*?

JH: We never had any discussion about the sex and violence one way or other. There was no discussion on any such issue as that. I did it the way that I thought would be best and tried to get a lot of humor into it. All the sex and violence were just kind of understood as a requirement of the genre.

RP: *The Big Bird Cage* addressed similar but also different social topics than *The Big Doll House*. Both films did this in politically incorrect ways. It simply moved from the lesbianism of Pam Grier's "Pretty soon, a girl gets strange desires, and it creeps on you like a disease, but it's curable" statement in *The Big Doll House* to the homosexuality of the guards led by Vic Diaz and Sig Haig's phony portrayal of a gay man in *The Big Bird Cage*. Instead of the nude females being sadistically tortured, we see an interracial relationship and the scene where a black woman, Grier, and a white man, Haig, do a smooching kiss, breaking a taboo at that time in *The Big Bird Cage*. Did you receive any backlash about portraying excessively exploitative stereotypes in the two films?

JH: I tried to turn stereotypes around for humor. Let me just say about the humor and homosexuality, one of the biggest areas where the picture played longest and earned its greatest attendance was in a gay neighborhood in Hollywood. So they were not offended.

RP: Your girlfriend at the time and producer of *The Big Bird Cage*, Jane Schaffer, suggested that she wanted you to move on from exploitation movies to more mainstream films. Why did you stay in the exploitation movie business?

JH: The films that I made were top-billed movies playing on their own level. Yes, Jane thought that I should go on to doing more mainstream films, and so did I. But directors get stereotyped the same way actors get stereotyped. You have a big hit playing a horror movie character as an actor, and the next thing you know, you're getting offers to play in more horror movies. The same thing is true for the director. It is very, very tough. If you have a little picture that does not make much money but gets good critical reviews, then you get a chance to be picked up by major studios. But when you have an exploitation movie that is a huge hit, then you become stereotyped as that type of director because those kinds of movies don't get great reviews. It is very hard to break out of that, and I didn't.

RP: Just as *The Big Doll House* put you on the map as arguably the greatest exploitation filmmaker, your films *The Big Doll House* and *The Big Bird Cage* elevated and accelerated the acting careers of Pam Grier, Sid Haig, Judith Brown, Roberta Collins, Brooke Mills, Anitra Ford and Vic Diaz. How much credit do you take for launching their great careers under your direction?

JH: You threw out a lot of names there, and some succeeded more than others. There was Sid Haig, of course, and Pam Grier. Pam had not done anything before I cast her. She did so well in *The Big Doll House* that she stayed on in the Philippines and did several other movies with other directors, local directors, before she did my sequel. It was her experience that made it possible for me when I got the opportunity to make the movie that eventually came out as *Coffy* (1973) to persuade the studios that she could handle the starring role and carry the picture herself and that she was the only black actress who could do it. It was because of the successful string of films that she had done that made it possible for me to persuade the studios to take her on.

RP: With *The Big Doll House*, *The Big Bird Cage*, *Coffy* and *Foxy Brown* (1974), each film being arguably the best of its kind, what things and/or people do you credit the most?

JH: Roger Corman for having the faith and confidence in me to allow me to just do what I wanted to do with *The Big Doll House*. Similarly, when I got the offers to do *Coffy* for American International Pictures, it was Larry Gordon who was the head of production, who believed in me and supported me against a lot of racism in the studios. Gordon shielded and supported me against these guys in the suits who thought they all knew better.

RP: What were the best things you learned from Roger Corman?

JH: Corman was pretty good himself at accomplishing a lot with very little money. The main thing I learned more than anything else was to get the maximum effect from a minimum of means. That helped me very much. He did not want to waste a nickel. Another thing I learned from him was how to make a movie look bigger on the screen than what you really had.

RP: Are there any other things you would like to say about your life and career in relation to Roger Corman?

JH: I credit him for—not just me but so many people—for giving me a break and opportunity to go out and shoot a movie without a lot of interference and trusting directors to do a good job. He did this knowing that, as a smart director himself, if anything would go wrong, he could step in and fix it at any time. He gave me these opportunities with minimum interference, and I learned from that, and I was really able to establish my own style. The pictures that I did on my own for other companies after Corman, those successes, really owe a lot to my experiences with Roger.

JONATHAN KAPLAN

Interview by Stephen B. Armstrong

STEPHEN B. ARMSTRONG: How did you get started as a filmmaker?

JONATHAN KAPLAN: I come from a family that was in the entertainment business. My uncle was Van Heflin, and my mother was an actress, Frances Kaplan. My father, Sol Kaplan, was a film composer who got blacklisted. So I grew up in the business. I thought it was not really a very wise choice to get into the business, just because it was so insecure, and, given the experience of the blacklist in particular, it didn't seem like the most stable of professions. When I was ten, Elia Kazan [Gadge], who had been a friend of my parents', would come and play poker at our house once a month or so. He had this little guillotine that clipped the ends of his cigars, and he used to let me use that. So as a very young kid I had vivid memories of Gadge.

He was the first major Hollywood figure to succumb to the Un-American Activities Committee and name names. He named my father, and so, out of guilt, I think, he cast me and my mother when I was ten as understudies in

43

the play *The Dark at the Top of the Stairs* by William Inge. He had directed my mother on Broadway in a couple of shows. It was a very strange and paranoid time, and he, Gadge, was sort of one of the main villains for having capitulated to the House Committee. We had moved to New York, and my father started working more or less as a ghostwriter. He wrote music for people but did not get the credit or the royalties. And my mother tried to work as an actress in live television, and she got two jobs right away when we got to New York. But both jobs were canceled when they asked her "Are you Mrs. Sol Kaplan?"

We were hurting very much financially, and in 1957, as I mentioned, Gadge gave us a job. My mother understudied Teresa Wright and Eileen Heckart, and I understudied the kid. That money obviously came in handy. Gadge, out of guilt, was extremely available to me. At ten, I understood some of what had gone on, but he was always Uncle Gadge. During the entire rehearsal process and the whole run of the show, I was at his side. He answered every question I had, and I just got to observe a great director directing a play by a great writer with great actors like Teresa Wright, Eileen Heckart and Pat Hingle.

So I really had this image of what a director was, and that's what I wanted to be, but I didn't think it was very likely. I went off to the University of Chicago and got involved in the political protests at the time, and I got kicked out for a sit-in against the war in Vietnam. So then I was back in New York, basically looking at being drafted. My draft status was 1-A, which meant you were very likely to be going off to the war. But they had this thing called the 2-S, which was a student deferment, and to qualify you had to be in college. I had just heard about the NYU film school.... It wasn't even a film school at that point, actually—rather, it was just sort of that you majored in film. "All you do is watch movies," I thought, "and you get your 2-S deferment?" So I ended up on Greene Street at NYU, on the eighth floor, where the NYU film school shared the premises with the Serbo-Croatian library. My first teacher was Harry Hurwitz. He also directed movies under the name "Harry Tampa." He was a wonderful teacher, who just basically let us do what we wanted to do. Instead of doing exercises with one-hundred-feet rolls of positive film, he had us all pool our film, and we made a what then was called a "nudie"—*These Raging Loins* (1968) it was called. And we each got to direct a scene. Some people dropped out, and some people didn't care, and so there were about four of us that actually made this movie. We got to make an actual low-budget exploitation picture in my first year at college. When the school found out they fired Harry.

Then Marty Scorsese came in, and I spent a year being in his class. It had an extremely collective point of view. Marty was pursuing his career, so sometimes he just would say, "Could somebody handle this for me?" I made a picture called "Stanley, Stanley." It was one of the five winners of what was then the National Student Film Festival in 1970. I won the comedy category.

So at the same time, I was working at the Fillmore. I was also editing for a show on PBS called *The Great American Dream Machine*, which had five editors—one was non-union, and that was me. I started as an assistant to the non-union editor because I was not in the IA [the International Alliance of Theatrical Stage Employees]. He left, so I took over for him. Producers would pitch and develop a couple of segments for each show. The executive producers would decide what was in the show and what wasn't. It was a great experience because it was fast and furious.

Sheila Nevins, who is now head of HBO Documentary and is a phenomenal, phenomenal producer—I got to work under her, and that was wonderful, though none of our segments ever made it to the show. But I sort of thought that I was going to be an editor. I really enjoyed it, and it was the one practical skill that I learned at NYU. There you actually learned how to work a Steenbeck and a Moviola and the splicer. I just found that to be fascinating. I was sort of hoping I could break my way into the union by getting my hours in New York to become an editor. Marty had gone out to do *Boxcar Bertha* for Roger Corman.

I came home from the Fillmore one night, and I was pretty tired; it had been a long weekend. The phone rang, and it was Roger Corman saying, "I've talked to Martin Scorsese, and he's recommended you. The director of the third in our Nurses cycle, *Night Call Nurses*, has had a disagreement with us. Creative differences. And my wife is producing it. Are you available to come out tomorrow and direct *Night Call Nurses*?" I thought it was a prank. I thought it was Jon Davison because Roger had been to NYU not that long before I got this call. I forget what picture he was promoting at that point, but we had a screening, and Roger spoke afterwards. I was completely raw when it came to Roger. I don't think Jon was. But the rest of us were really shocked by how straight Roger was. He sounded like an announcer, and he spoke in complete sentences. We sort of expected this guy to have long hair, this biker type, because of the pictures he'd made.

Jon did a very good Roger Corman imitation, and I thought it was him pranking me. So I just said something and hung up. The phone rang again. I picked it up, and it was Roger. He said, "Young man, there are people lining up from here to London who would jump at this opportunity. I'm serious about this." He hadn't seen "Stanley, Stanley." He hadn't even seen anything I'd done. He hadn't seen any of my other student work. But he just took Marty's word for it because he liked Marty. I found out years later that Marty had given him several names, and Roger just happened to call me first. He said, "Can you come tomorrow?" And I said, "Well, yeah." The first thing that came to mind was I didn't drive, and I said, "Listen, I'm going to need someone to drive me around Los Angeles because I don't drive." And he said, "I'm not asking you to be the transportation captain. I'm asking you if you can direct." And I said, "Oh, sure. Yeah, I can direct." So next day I was out in L.A. The rest is history.

SA: You were to work with a script from George Armitage, right?

JK: That's correct. But we rewrote the script for *Night Call Nurses*. I mean Roger basically told me there had been creative differences between George and Julie and did not go into detail; he just said that they had some issues with the script. They didn't use the word "issues" then; that was not colloquial then. But he just said, "We have some notes, and I'll need you to rewrite the script." He said this on the phone, and he said that he would pay me. "I understand you're quite a good editor," he said. And I said, "Oh, thank you." "You'll edit the film, and you'll direct it. And also I'll need you to rewrite the script, and I'll pay you $9 thousand." The amount bugged me, but.... So, eventually, a co-editor was brought on, Alan Collins, who's a great guy. After my first meeting with Roger, I was completely terrified, I had no idea what the fuck to do. Roger had told me: "You have thirteen days to do this picture and $75 thousand." So I talked to Jon, and Jon said, "Look at the pictures." I looked at the other nurses pictures and some other New World pictures, and I realized very quickly that how you get this done is you do a lot of scenes in one shot, or one shot and a pop, and one little piece of coverage or something. And that's how you make the schedule.

Jon was obviously my guru in terms of all things Corman. I asked him to come out and rewrite the script. And he came out with Danny Opatoshu, who was a classmate of ours at NYU. Roger wanted me to start casting and go into preproduction immediately while rewriting the script. Danny and Jon rewrote it while I was casting during the day and finding locations and so forth.

New World was a well-oiled machine in the sense that there was guaranteed employment. Not for luxurious wages, but there was project-to-project guaranteed employment for technicians and production staff. The support staff knew the ropes. I wasn't acting like a pictorial director or that I had a vision. I understood that my job was to deliver for Roger. The first time I met him, he showed me the poster that had been made for *Night Call Nurses*—there were four women pictured. He basically said, "We need to cast a blonde-blue-eyed-fair-young woman. She'll be the comedic subplot. And then we have a brunette, and that'll be the action-kinky subplot. And then we have a person of color, and that's our socially conscious political subplot." I said, "And what's the fourth subplot?" And he said, "Oh, no. That's just a model. She's not actually in the movie." He also said, "You need to shoot total nudity from the waist up. Nudity from behind. No pubic hair. Go to work. You'll meet with Julie, and you'll rewrite the script. Go to work." I understood what the priorities were. I was not making a Jonathan Kaplan movie; I was making a Roger Corman movie.

When I first met Roger and started working with him, he'd directed, let's say, seventy-five pictures. I thought: "If this is low-rent-bottom-shelf filmmaking in Hollywood, this is great. It's got to be amazing as you get more money for the budget and you work your way up in the system." Roger was the best producer I ever worked for in terms of understanding what a director does. He has his own self-confidence, and his own knowledge of where to apply the pressure for what he needs while letting you have all the freedom within those requirements. I'd never get so much freedom again. It was an ideal situation for a first feature film—where you feel that these people know what they're doing and they have confidence in you. They're very specific about what they need: they need the nudity; they need the elements that the pictures promise their audience. But once those elements are delivered, everything else—it's up to you. It's whatever you want, within the constraints of the schedule and the budget.

But I was sort of curious, wondering if he was going to teach me something about how he wanted me to go about this or that. And then he said, "We're going to have lunch, and I'm going to go over the visual style with you." We had lunch at this place on Sunset Boulevard, and he purposely asked for a certain table. We went to this table in the corner of the restaurant, and he said, "So if you were going to shoot this scene between you and me having this conversation, where would you put the camera?" And I just said, "Ahh.... Here." And he said, "Well, actually, if you put it here, in the corner, you have the whole restaurant behind us. That's where you should shoot your master from; that will give you the depth and the production value of the location. And then you shoot your covers based on that."

He emphasized screen directions, too. "Make sure that this person on the left is looking at this person on the right, and that they're...." And he gave me a very quick primer on screen direction, which is vastly important. So many directors get it wrong. That was it: that was the conversation about visual style. The information, about lenses, for example, I knew; I understood that the higher the millimeter the more of a portrait lens it was, the less depth of field there was. And that to make the women look good, you want to shoot them with a longer lens, a fifty or above, and try to shoot the masters and the establishing shots in the wide angle lens to get the most out of the production and out of the location. And that was it.

SA: That was the primer?

JK: That was it. And that is as articulate and economic a conversation about something that people can make careers out of. It's really all you need to know. Establish the geography, let the audience know where they are, where the characters are in relation to each other and how to make people look good. That was pretty much it. He understood that you learn by doing, and he just wanted to give me the confidence and to express his confidence in me. He showed me how he prepared because I asked him.

He showed me with a napkin and a pen how he does overviews or the bird's-eye view of the set or the location, and how to indicate where the camera angles are, where the people are and so forth. What he said, basically, was "A lot of the teaching that I'm seeing that people are getting in film school is about where to put the camera, which, obviously, is a major decision. But you have to also think about where the people move. And I find it's more helpful to work out where the people move first and then decide about where the camera goes based on where the people go. Because the actors will want some say. They'll want to have some say in where they're moving about. They're not robots. You can't just tell them 'On this line you go here, and on that line you go there.' You have your preparation in mind, and you have your floor plans. Then you present it to the actors as a suggestion where you want them to move and when you want them to move and how you want to block it. But you have to be open to their input. If you block yourself into a camera position and have no flexibility, then you're asking for trouble."

SA: Aside from Roger's influence over the way you handled framing and lighting and blocking, were you allowing other filmmakers' work to influence you? When I see *Night Call Nurses* and when I see *The Student Teachers* and even *Truck Turner* (1974), it looks to me like there's some French New Wave in it. Who were the directors you were emulating back then, if any?

JK: Hitchcock, Ford, Hawks, George Stevens and Capra. I loved movies and watched a lot of movies. But I don't consciously work like "Let me do this like this. Let me do this like that. This'll be..." Of the French New Wave directors, Truffaut was my favorite. I'm not a big Godard fan. For me, visual style evolves out of the material. It's not about imposing your visual style on every picture, the same visual style, just so that you can be an auteur. It's all about telling a story and what's the best way to tell a story. It's just about entertainment, telling a story. And subjectivity. Character subjectivity—to me that was what certainly Hitchcock was the master of. You have to decide which story you're telling. You have to decide the point of view, your point of view toward the material—and which character you want the audience to identify with. In any given scene, you have to decide from whose point of view you want this scene to be playing. Not necessarily a POV shot or a subjective through-the-eyes-of-a character shot, though obviously that's a tool and a very important one. Rather it entails thinking in terms of "Where's the master? Where do you place the camera for the wide shot? Are you looking at the character you want the audience to be identifying with, or are you back over there looking at what they're seeing?"

Similarly with lens choices. It's *like* a character's point of view, like when you're tracking with someone the obvious choice is to track in front of them and see their face, which is the shot you need. But it's also that you want to see what they're seeing, and that could be a straight-tracking-shot point of view without them in the frame. Or it could be over their shoulder or behind their body and walking with them so that you're seeing what they're seeing. And you're also seeing them in the frame.

If you're saying "Oh, this is a visual style that I like. I want to make this look like this" or "I want to use this lens with this filter" that's ass-backwards to me. You have to know "What's the story? Who's the character that I want the audience to identify with? Whose scene is this, in terms of how I want us to react, to take in the scene the same way the character takes in the scene."

It's all about point of view. It's all about telling a story, I directed a picture called *Heart Like a Wheel* (1983) about Shirley Muldowney. There's a scene in there where Bonnie Bedelia plays the lead, Shirley Muldowney. It's her son's birthday party, and his father, her estranged husband, she's waiting for him to call her, and he hasn't called. It's just her and her mother and her son celebrating the birthday. Her love interest at the time, Connie Kalitta, is played by Beau Bridges. She goes into the kitchen to do something. The camera stays with her in the kitchen. And we hear Beau Bridges arrive with a girlfriend, and we watch Bonnie react to just the sound. We don't see Beau yet. We don't see the girlfriend. We just hear him come in. He's larger than life, and he's greeting her son, her sister and her mother. We hear this other female voice, his girlfriend's. And then we track with Bonnie as she exits the kitchen and comes into the dining room, and we see her boyfriend, Beau Bridges, and his new girlfriend, along with Bonnie.

So it's completely subjective from the point of view of the character Shirley Muldowney. The visual is late. It's as if you're sitting there just hearing this, like she's listening to a radio play. Then she walks out into the room and we are in her point of view. We see this woman for the first time when Shirley sees her for the first time. That's what I mean by "subjectivity."

SA: I understand. Rethinking my own understanding here, because I guess what made the *Night Call Nurses* seem almost French to me is that it's almost like a perfect blend of art house and genre, like *Shoot the Piano Player* (1960) or something. And yet, when I asked you who were the directors that mattered most, it was these commercial, contractual studio directors. It's just very interesting. But, of course, Truffaut and Godard and all those *nouvelle vague* guys were looking at those American directors, as well.

JK: Exactly, exactly. When I was coming up and Allan was and Jon was and Joe was and Paul Bartel, too, the whole sort of academic film world and any kind of film scholarship were all driven by the French. Godard and Truffaut and Rohmer and so forth. That was what was in vogue. The first things Harry Hurwitz, however, showed us were Chaplin shorts. And Marty, the first thing he showed us was *The Searchers* (1956). At the time, John Wayne was the enemy because of the Vietnam war, so the idea that here was this film that we were supposed to take seriously, what Marty was saying was one of the greatest movies ever made, was a John Wayne western directed by John Ford. Harry and Marty sort of kicked the French out of us. Not that they disrespected the French, but it was like "This is who these guys are talking about. These are the directors these guys are talking about." I was not one of the great advocates of the French New Wave because I love American movies. To have these guys at NYU constantly advocating these pictures by these directors.... It was great.

SA: Thanks for not crushing me about the French influence. So what happened in the interim between *Night Call Nurses* and your follow-up for New World, *The Student Teachers*?

JK: Well, I just left. I never let go of my New York apartment. I finished *Night Call Nurses*, finished editing it, and Roger was pleased. I figured: "Okay, that was that. This picture's pretty dreadful, and I'm going to go back to New York and get in the damn Editors Guild." Then I got a call from Julie in the late summer, saying that *Night Call Nurses* had broken house records in Tallahassee, and that Roger was very pleased with the box office. So, in her words, he wanted to do the same picture again—but with teachers. And she said, "The title is *The Student Teachers*." And I said, "Oh, so the tagline is 'Enter their course!'" She told that to Roger, and he loved it. It was like: "Kaplan really understands what we're doing here."

So we were back at it. Roger was very involved in the script, and since we were not starting with a rewrite, but starting from scratch, there was more to deal with. Roger basically functions like this on a script. He would have his legal pad, and he'd have, say, thirty notes. And you come in with the writers. It was Danny Opatoshu on this one, who had also worked on *Night Call Nurses*. We'd come in, and there'd be these thirty notes. We'd say, "Okay," and we'd go back and do ten of them. And then the next draft would come in from Roger, and then there'd be twenty notes about the twenty we didn't do. And by the time we were done with the script, we'd done all thirty notes.

Julie was producing again, and the only time we heard from Roger was regarding cast. He had one request, and we cast a Ford model as one of the teachers. That was it. Everything else was about budget and schedule. The next time I saw Roger, in terms of any input into the picture, came when we did the first cut. He would always look at the first day's dailies. Both *Night Call Nurses* and *The Student Teachers* were shot in color, but in those days, it was cheaper just to have the dailies printed in black and white. And we'd only have the printed dailies screened on the first day's shoot. Roger would come to dailies and watch it with us on the screen at a screening room on Sunset Boulevard. Roger would just look at those dailies and say, "Fine, everything's fine." And that would be that. "Go ahead. Keep going." And we just went about our merry way. I had told him when we first started I wanted to try to make it more kinetic than *Night Call Nurses*, and he was fine with that.

SA: And Dick Miller? He is one of these actors, one of the faces of New World. You worked with him, too.

JK: Julie had said for *Night Call Nurses*, "There's this actor, Dick Miller. And he's worked with Roger in the past. But you don't have to use him. And he doesn't come in and read."

I had mentioned it to Davison, and he said, "Dick Miller? Of course, you've got to get Dick Miller in here. You've got to put Dick in the picture." He brought me up to speed on Dick Miller. Dick came in, finally, after some cajoling. He came in, and he said, "Look, I don't read well. I don't audition well." We read through the scene, and he was pretty stiff. I said, "You're right. You don't audition well." So Jon said, "I'm going to write a part for him." He wrote the part in *Night Call Nurses*, the masher character. And we had to get a Jensen Motors automobile into the movie because Roger had some deal. There were two products, actually, that we had to show in the movie: the Jensen automobile and a Bulova watch. Roger had some deal with them. So Jon said, "He can be the guy, what they used to call a masher, that guy who makes passes." So Jon wrote that scene in *Night Call Nurses* for Dick, and we cast him. And we had a great time. I used Dick as many times as I could after that.

SA: He was in those two movies that you made for New World. And then he's in *The Slams* (1973), and he was in *Truck Turner*, too.

JK: Right, right. And in *Truck Turner* he brought his own wardrobe. He wore the pink jacket, which you'll see a lot in Dick Miller's performance.

SA: Yeah. That's a good film. I remember Allan Arkush turning me onto that a couple of years ago. And I have it on DVD in my house—

JK: Oh, good.

SA: Yeah. So *The Student Teachers* turned out well. I don't know about its commercial performance.

JK: The formula worked. Between the drive-ins and the triple features and double features, in the cities, it did really well. It didn't cost anything. It cost one-hundred-twenty-five grand or so.

SA: Okay. Did you just take new job offers? Is that how your career progressed at that point, or—?

JK: Yeah, well, I got *The Slams* because Gene Corman, Roger's brother, came to see the cast-and-crew screening of *The Student Teachers*. And he and his wife walked out after about, I don't know, thirty minutes. I was freaked out. I thought, "Oh, I guess.... " I knew he was considering me for a picture. And I said, "Ah, I guess I'm not getting that job." I still really expected just to be done and to be editing in New York. But Gene called me the next day and offered me *The Slams*. And I said, "I was sort of not expecting this call because you walked out of the screening." He said, "Well, no. I just saw what you did with the black subplot, and that's all I needed to see because this is a blaxploitation picture starring Jim Brown. So if you want to do it, we have to have a lunch with Jim Brown, and if he signs off, then you've got the job. So that lead to *The Slams*, which lead to *Truck Turner*. A guy who I went to NYU with, Kent Friedman, he and I had started collaborating after that, and we wrote the treatment for *White Line Fever* (1975), which we submitted to Columbia Pictures the weekend that *Truck Turner* opened. *Truck Turner* did great business in Chicago and Detroit. Back in those days, it took until Monday to get the grosses. The treatment had just landed on Peter Guber's desk at Columbia, and he saw that *White Line Fever*—that it's about truck drivers. *Truck Turner* is right then setting records in Detroit and Chicago, and so they bought the treatment thinking that *Truck Turner* was about truck drivers!

For *White Line Fever* I wanted to do a Leone Western, with trucks instead of horses. I'd been writing on all the films I'd worked on except for *The Slams*. *The Student Teachers* had a formula. Roger is the auteur of that movie. And Roger is the auteur of all the New World Pictures in terms of the parameters that he sets. But *White Line Fever* was the first movie that started from scratch with no parameters, except we knew we wanted to make an action picture. So in terms of visual style, that owed a lot to Leone.

SA: When you left New World, there was no bad blood? You just moved on and—

JK: Listen, if Roger called me today, I'd do a movie for him. I don't think I would be as good at what I do if it weren't for Roger. It's a charmed life to have had Kazan and Henry Hurwitz, Scorsese and Roger. If I had not met Roger and gotten the opportunity from him, had him show the confidence in me... It was not a bullshit kind of "Oh, I'm a big fan" kind of confidence, you know. It was genuine, backed by his own self-interest. By giving me the job, he was saying, "I trust this guy. I think this guy can deliver this. And as long as I put the pressure on him at these points...." " And it was a gentle pressure from him. "These are the points that I need to enter into the equation to make sure I'm getting what I want. But aside from that you're free to do whatever you want."

That's something that very few people get, a chance to try something and then see how it's working. It's only by doing that that you can do this and that you can learn that, and it's wonderful. It gives you the confidence to be able to express yourself and to trust yourself. The emphasis on preparation was vastly important, with emphasis on the director's first responsibility, which is to the economics, because you have to deliver this on-time and on schedule. These are the elements that he requires in order to ensure the movie makes money. Once that was satisfied, I could do anything I want with all the other decisions. That's a great way to begin your career.

SA: That almost seems like a perfect note to end the interview. But if I could just press you a little bit-

JK: No, go ahead. Go ahead.

SA: Not press. Just ask about the acting in, say, *Hollywood Boulevard*. You were in *Cannonball!*, too, right?

JK: And also a one-scene part in *Piranha*. I was a gas station attendant, and Dennis Dugan was in the scene. Two directors in one scene.

SA: So was that just to help out some friends? To have some fun? How did that go with acting in these pictures?

JK: The beauty of New World was that it was a genuine community. We all collaborated on each other's stuff. The editing rooms were in the same place, we were all up at New World in the offices there, and we all had shared crew. We weren't rooting for each other to fail, which is what I call the "Hollywood disease." There was a genuine camaraderie. If Jon made a bet with Roger that he could make this picture *Hollywood Boulevard* for this amount of money, for instance, we would all show up and work for nothing and just do it because we'd get to see each other and laugh our asses off.

It was mostly about just cracking up. And Roger has the same sense of humor. Roger would tell stories on himself. There was one time on *Student Teachers*, and I had written this line in the description that says, "Cut to Valley High School, to corridor. It's wall-to-wall people, wall-to-wall students." I get there, and there are six extras. I say to Julie, "It says 'wall-to-wall.' How am I going to shoot this corridor scene?" And she said, "Call Roger." So I present the problem to Roger, and he says, "Use a long lens. You have someone running around the camera, they take off their jacket, they put on their jacket. And you just keep the shots as condensed as possible on a long lens with lots of movement." I said, "Really?" He said, "I shot the war between Greece and Italy with five extras and a bush. Surely you can shoot a high school corridor." We both laughed.

JON DAVISON

Interview by Stephen B. Armstrong

Stephen B. Armstrong: Tell me about your early interest in movies and how you were able to turn that into a pretty fascinating career.

Jon Davison: Well, it wasn't just an early interest in movies. It was an early interest in Roger Corman. In 1957, I was eight years old, and my brother and I went to the Century Theatre in Audubon, New Jersey. We saw *Attack of the Crab Monster* sand *Not of This Earth* on a double bill. I remember spending quite a bit of time in the men's room, especially during *Not of This Earth*, which terrified me. That was my first experience with Roger Corman, and he has haunted and delighted me throughout my entire life. For my high school term paper, which I think you had to do when you were a junior, I wrote it on Roger Corman and dedicated it to Dick Miller. I then went to NYU film school, and one of my professors was Marty Scorsese. At some point while I was there, I guess Roger called Haig Manoogian, the head of the school, and asked for a recommendation for directors. Haig recommended Marty, and he directed *Boxcar Bertha* for Roger. Then Julie Corman approached Marty and said that she needed a director for *Night Call Nurses*, and he recommended my friend and classmate Jonathan Kaplan. Danny Opatoshu and I went to L.A. to rewrite the script for *Night Call Nurses*. We weren't getting paid or anything: but the deal I made with Jonathan was that while I would work for free, "You have to hire Dick Miller." Dick Miller had not worked for Roger for years. Jonathan didn't know who Dick Miller was, but he ended up hiring him.

After *Night Call Nurses*, Roger offered me $1 thousand to write *India Doll House*. I took the money and went back to New Jersey and split it with Joe Dante and Michael Wakely. The three of us wrote the script. I used my $333 to buy a plane ticket to L.A. to deliver it to Roger. As luck would have it, his director of advertising had just committed suicide—so I got offered the job. That put me in charge of advertising and publicity as there was no other person in the department: I was it. So I stayed in Los Angeles and started working there. It consumed my life. I lived in the office. I immediately called up Allan Arkush and Joe Dante. I asked them to please come help me and do the trailers and TV spots. Joe was resistant because he was editing *Film Bulletin* magazine. But the publisher of the magazine was going broke and had stopped paying Joe a salary. So Joe finally said, "Listen, if I can't get a salary next month, I'll come out and work for you cutting trailers. The magazine went under and, fortunately for me, Joe came out.

SA: Before we go further, I'd like to mention that I interviewed Paul Chihara recently. He did the music for *Death Race 2000* and *I Never Promised You a Rose Garden* and worked on *Submersion of Japan* (1973).

JD: What does Paul Chihara do now?

SA: He's a professor specializing in composition at NYU. He was at UCLA. When I introduced *Death Race* at a screening in the Bowery a year and a half ago, he showed up with his wife. I find him to be a great person.

Very helpful and informative, with good memories of New World during what I thought were the best years before the lumberyard purchase.

JD: I was gone before they bought the lumberyard, but that struck me as artistically a great mistake to have these cheap movies become set-bound. Roger used to go on about free production value in the 1970s. He'd say, "Go out and get free production value! Go to the beach! Go to Venice! Go to parades! Go to the park!" It really opened the pictures up—the nurses and teachers pictures of the 1970s, those movies. Everything was on location. There were no sets. Even if you needed an office, you went to someone's office; nothing ever got built. It added visual production value to these pictures— that really was a plus. Once they started building sets, it just seemed like such a mistake to me.

SA: There is a bit of a cult following around the James Cameron pictures made for New World. *Battle Beyond the Stars*, for instance.

JD: Well, in a science fiction picture, you're inside a spaceship. You're not going to find a practical location for that. But for offices and other places, to shoot them at a studio with no money, it didn't seem like a good idea to me.

SA: Tell me what the workday was like when you were at New World. I take it you would stop in and work on trailers with Allan Arkush and Joe Dante. Then you might dart off and get involved with something else—story development with Frances Doel, maybe—or writing the posters?

JD: Well, the editing room early on was in Hollywood. It would have several locations eventually. New World originally was right next to Tower Records on 8831 Sunset Boulevard. I had an office there. Roger had the penthouse suite of the building, and my office was next to his. There was a swinging door between the two offices. I always left it open, about six inches, so I could hear what Roger was saying on the phone and in his meetings.

I virtually listened to every conversation this guy had for years. It taught me everything I knew about movies at the time. I'd get up in the morning, and I'd go to the office. The phone was always ringing, so I'd take a lot of phone calls. I tried to get things done. I was in charge of post-production, as well as advertising, so I was on the phone with the lab a lot. We used to go to the lab almost every day, mostly at MGM's facility in Culver City. I'd swing by the editing room to see cuts of trailers, but mostly I'd head to the lab. I didn't really develop any scripts for Roger, aside from *Hollywood Boulevard* (1976), and I worked on *Piranha* somewhat. But Roger was always generating the material. He would come up with the idea for a picture, then he'd have Frances write it over the weekend. Then they would hire another writer to do the polish. Roger would write copious notes on legal pads. Roger and Frances really developed all of the material. Before I got there, Larry Woolner, who was the first general sales manager at New World Pictures, would also come up with some ideas for movies, after talking to the sub-distributors around the country. But once Larry Woolner left, Roger generated all of the pictures.

SA: Tell me about story development for *Hollywood Boulevard*. And the famous bet involving you and Roger and Allan and Joe.

JD: Well, by this time, I was also the head of production, on top of the other work. And the average low-budget New World picture, the nurses and teachers movies, were costing about $ 75 thousand. I figured that if I told Roger I could make a picture for $50 thousand by using stock footage, then he would probably go for it. I pitched the idea at Ciro's restaurant in West Hollywood during lunch, and he did indeed go for this because it was going to be $25 cheaper than any New World movie. That is what got us going. Roger said, "Well, you three can make this movie as long as it doesn't interfere with the work you're doing for the trailers and advertising. You can go ahead and do it." It was only a ten-day movie, so it probably didn't interfere much with the trailers.

SA: Were you on set? I know that a lot of *Hollywood Boulevard* was shot outdoors. Allan and Joe would have to coordinate about who shot what and who shot when and who shot where since they were codirecting the picture. One person would do his shot, then the other would do his, right? Were you there at all?

JD: Yeah, I was there all the time. I was there at the call and left after the wrap. That movie was so cheap. Joe was the one who had sound, and Allan didn't have any sound. You're right. They wouldn't shoot at the same place at the same time.

SA: As I understand it, Joe and Allan would go back and cut trailers when they weren't making the film.

JD: They took two weeks off, made that picture, and then pretty much were just back in the trailer department afterward.

SA: How did *Hollywood Boulevard* change your daily routine?

JD: It just got me out of the office for two weeks, and that was pretty much it. I went back to my job in production. I think I was still also doing the advertising and publicity. Around that time, we had a couple of other people I hired come in to the department: Todd McCarthy and Joe McBride. They were both reviewers for the trade papers. They had offices downstairs. This must have been after we moved from Sunset Boulevard to Brentwood. Roger still occupies that building to this very day. At that point, Todd and Joe were writing all of the press releases and press books, especially for the foreign films. I used to have to write all the press material, and I think I did that right through *Hollywood Boulevard* until those two thankfully came on.

SA: You'd write these knockout taglines to promote the films. You came up with the one for one of the blaxploitation movies—

JD: "TNT Jackson: she'll put you in traction." Yeah, I used to write all the radio spots and record all the radio spots. I used to write the trailer narrations. Joe and Allan would both come up with great lines, too. It was the three of us who wrote the ad copy. We also made two or three sixty-second spots, and a bunch of thirtys and some tens and twentys. The ads were all laid out by a guy named Ed Carlin, who was also a movie producer, who produced his own pictures. I hired a guy by the name of John Solie quite a bit, and he did a lot of the artwork for the posters. He's got a website, and you can look him up. He's still painting. I think he's in Arizona or New Mexico. He was terrific and really funny. I'd send down the leading ladies to his studio, and I think they always had a great time doing the posters. I can't remember the photographic guy I used to hire.

Curtis Hanson would come by. He had done a picture called *Sweet Kill* in 1972, which was a pretty good picture that dropped dead. He was renting me a little bungalow in Hollywood, where I lived, which I think his mother owned. I suggested that we reissue the picture under a different title, *The Arousers*. That was another one of my jobs. I had to come up with titles for pictures, especially after the initial opening—we'd always change titles over the weekend. We called the picture *The Arousers*, and I did a new campaign, which had a sexual stimulation test to be given to everyone entering the theater. We shot new scenes in the little bungalow I rented, sex scenes as I recall, to kind of juice up the picture.

I would stay in the office on a Friday night. The pictures opened on a Friday night typically. They only played in one territory at a time. We had thirteen sub-distributors around the country. You'd make about fifty to one-hundred prints of a picture, normally, in the early-to-mid 1970s. You'd move the prints around the country. On the first opening, you'd stay in the office late, and you'd start calling the theaters to see what the grosses were. An hour or two after the picture opened, you knew what you had. Either you were going to be there all weekend coming up with a new title and new title campaign because the picture had dropped dead, or you could say, "Thank

God! We got six-hundred bucks at the local passion pit, and that's going to be good enough."

SA: You left New World. Why?

JD: I left because I had just finished *Grand Theft Auto*. I always did the sound mixes on the movies. When I say I did them, I was at the mixing studio, and I ran the mixes—unless the director wanted or needed to do it. This was before magnetic tape, so everything was recorded direct to 35mm negative in one-thousand foot rolls. If there was a mistake you had to start over—you had to start the reel over. On *Grand Theft Auto*, the last reel was this big demolition derby—nonstop action the whole reel. I'd hired Richard Anderson, who did a fantastic job with the tracks. He'd hired some fantastic young kids, who probably didn't get credit. Roger never let you get overtime on the mixing stage. You generally had one or two days to mix a movie. This last reel was so complicated I needed an extra one or two hours of time and a half to complete the film and make it sound as good as it could. I called Roger at home, and I said, "Roger, I need another hour of time and a half to make the track really good." He said, "No." So I decided, "That's it. I'm leaving this place because if he doesn't care about the movies, then I'm not going to make them here." I told him the next day that I was leaving. I don't know how long I stayed after that but probably not more than a week or so. It was a good thing. It was too much work, and it was killing me. Then he hired me back to do *Piranha*.

SA: How did you move on to big studios? You served as producer on *Airplane!* for Paramount.

JD: I was doing pre-production on *Piranha* when the Zuckers brought me the first draft of *Airplane!* When I read it, I said, "Boy, this is terrific. I'd love to produce it, but you have to wait until I finish *Piranha*. I think it took several years after I finished *Piranha* to actually get the money to produce it. Once I did *Airplane!*, even my father stopped bugging me to go to law school.

SA: How did the experiences of working on these bigger pictures differ from working on the zilch-budget operations of the sort that Roger oversaw?

JD: At the very end of my career I did a couple more cheap movies. I did one for Roger, *Searchers 2.0* (2007), that Alex Cox directed, and I think that was a ten-day picture. I started my career with a ten-day picture for Roger and ended it with a ten-day picture for Roger. There's something to be said for movies that are short and sweet. You don't get sick of them. I loved doing low-budget movies.

SA: Do they present opportunities for more creativity since the budget and the economic stakes are not so high?

JD: I don't know. I mean, you have to design the movie for the money you have, which Roger always did when he was directing. You can be just as creative with $100 million as you can with a million.

SA: You got to meet the person who meant so much to you as a child— how did coming into Roger's sphere change or influence you?

JD: Roger Corman was the best thing that ever happened to me in my life. I wanted to be a producer as a child for some weird reason, and I followed this career. I just couldn't believe it when I got to go out and meet him. I remember when he offered me the job of being in charge of advertising. We were having dinner at the Old World Restaurant in West Hollywood with Jonathan Kaplan and Julie [Corman]. I started telling Roger about how I collected prints of his movies, and he was pleased. I remember Julie was somewhat taken aback by this, thinking, 'He's stealing my husband's movies.'

But Roger was quite pleased by it all. I think that helped me, my knowledge of his work, to get the job in the first place.

SA: What is it like to work for someone that you at some point idolized?

JD: I still have an enormous love and affection for the guy. He is still as charming and friendly and open as he was when I met him in the early 1970s. Roger is really cheap, but he really is an honest, open and funny guy. He walks around with a big smile, and now I'm sure he tells the same stories over and over again. He was a pleasure to work for, even though I was upset that he wouldn't let me spend another hour in the mix. But Roger used to say that "Anybody who does more than a couple of pictures for me is probably not very talented because after a couple of pictures they should probably be moving on." I heard Roger say this numerous times, and so I just moved on.

DICK MILLER, WITH LAINIE MILLER

Interview by Stephen B. Armstrong

STEPHEN B. ARMSTRONG: Tell me about your relationship with Roger Corman—you worked with him as both an actor and a writer.

DICK MILLER: I always thought Roger was one of the nicest guys in the business. We got along great. We didn't socialize any—more of a business contact, really—but he was just great.

SA: How about Joe Dante? You've been in several movies that he made, including *Hollywood Boulevard* and *Piranha*.

DM: Well, I got along with him, too. He was also another guy who is just too nice to be in the business. I seemed to work with a lot of directors who if I worked with them once they wanted to work with me again. At the time it didn't seem like a lot, but as I look back, I can see that I did a lot of work for certain directors.

SA: Why do you think directors like Joe Dante and Jonathan Kaplan, and Allan Arkush, too, called you back again and again?

DM: I had the reputation of being "One-take Miller."

SA: What makes a character actor successful? Why is it you that you were able to play all these different roles in the movies made for New World, and how was this different, say, from being a leading man?

DM: I *was* a leading man. I starred in a lot of pictures, more than a dozen, for Roger, Joe and the other guys. You reach a period when you're going to make it as a leading man or become—I don't like the term—a *character actor*. Being a character actor limits you to small parts, to one part that you do over and over again. I always seemed to be doing everything. Good guys, bad guys. It wasn't the same. I never saw myself as a character actor. I thought of myself sometimes as a leading man who was getting smaller parts.

SA: I was thinking of a character actor as someone who has tremendous range and can sort of dissolve into different parts and be this guy or that guy. Good, bad…

DM: No. A character actor is usually noted for one part. He plays it over and over and over again.

SA: Why do you that think you were so good at playing different roles in the New World movies, at assuming different characters so easily?

DM: Because I'd lived a lot.

SA: Any anecdotes come to mind about the movies you made for New World Pictures? *Rock 'N' Roll High School*, for instance?

DM: We had a lot of fun on that. The Ramones! I gave them a lot of trouble. I remember they were telling me not to wear my uniform. I was playing a police captain or something. They said, "Don't wear your jacket out there so you won't be seen. You may get shot." It was a rough neighborhood where we were shooting.

SA: Any other thoughts maybe about Roger or Joe? Jonathan Kaplan, Julie Corman, John Sayles?

DM: I seem to have gotten along with these people just fine.

LAINIE MILLER: He's highly respected by these guys. Dick doesn't like to say it—I'm going to say it—some of these people who worked with Roger and were of note themselves seemed to feel that Dick is a good luck charm. They wanted him in their pictures for that reason. Dick is a little shy about this, so he's not saying it. It's the truth. I hear it from Joe. I've heard it from Jonathan. I hear it from all of them.

SA: And it's true. Look at all the great movies Mr. Miller's been in. He really made moves like *The Student Teachers* and *Piranha* better than they would have otherwise been.

MICHAEL PRESSMAN

Interview by Stephen B. Armstrong

STEPHEN B. ARMSTRONG: I love *The Great Texas Dynamite Chase* (1976). How did you wind up making it for New World?

MICHAEL PRESSMAN: I had some long-lasting friendships with a lot of the people who worked at New World, but I was actually able to make the movie outside of the New World banner. I grew up in New York. I came from a theater arts family. My father was an acting teacher, an actor and a theater director, and my mother was a dancer. I went to Carnegie Mellon for theater and then transferred to California Institute of the Arts in Los Angeles and studied for three years with a brilliant film director named Alexander Mackendrick, who'd made *Sweet Smell of Success* (1957). I was one of the first graduating classes at CalArts in 1973, and I went there the first year the school opened. I was in the first of the group of students to graduate.

I was a childhood friend of Jonathan Kaplan. Jonathan had graduated from NYU and come out to L.A. He was several years older. When I got out of film school, and I was struggling doing odd jobs, Jonathan said, "I'll get you an introduction to Roger Corman." So I saw some of the movies, I met with Roger, and I had a short film that I made at film school that he viewed, and he said, "Okay, he can direct." I came into a meeting. I pitched a nurses' movie. He was still making those nurses films. Corman said, "Why don't you start working?" I did that for several months. Then I read that the film was announced, and then the film was canceled, and I was despondent. I called Jonathan, and he said, "Go back again. Just go back again, and come up with a new idea."

I got together with a friend, and we went back and pitched him *The Great Texas Dynamite Chase*, which was originally titled *Dynamite Women*. And he said, "I'll distribute it." At that time, negative pick-ups were very common. Roger Corman gave us a guarantee of, if I remember correctly, one-third negative pick-up. How it worked was—if somebody invested $10 thousand, they would get one third of their money back. This friend of mine gave us roughly $75 thousand, and we made the film for around $200 thousand. A whole year passed with us trying to find investors, and there was a lot of interest in the Roger Corman movies and in a four-to-one tax shelter, which allowed for someone to invest ten and write off forty. It was a tax incentive in L.A. at the time to invest in independent movies.

My friend David Irving, a producer, who subsequently became the head of the NYU film school, and I got an office, and we ran a little ad in the *L.A. Times* that said, "If you invest in this movie, you have the chance to double your money." I remember my lawyer calling me: "You can't say that. You're going to get sued." We were still in our twenties. We didn't know what we were doing. But we got a lawyer who helped us with all the paperwork, and we founded a company. I had friends who invested, and I had an ex-brother-in-law, the famous Nick Meyer, the writer-director, he invested $10 thousand. And we got the movie made. We had a certain amount more freedom than the others. I had meetings with Roger, and he approved casting. He approved Claudia Jennings. But we put together our own team and used a lot of the people who were working there at New World. We shot for twenty-five days, and I heard they were making the films in eighteen and twenty days. We had opportunities and challenges that were different than what the normal New World restrictions typically were. But we followed things pretty clearly. Roger came to a screening and approved the film, and that was that.

The film got rave reviews. I was sort of blown away by the success of it. I had no idea what the impact would be. It launched my career very quickly. I found myself within a year's time directing the sequel to The Bad News Bears (1976)—The Bad News Bears in Breaking Training (1977)—and that was a big studio movie with a $3-million-dollar budget. I was sort of jettisoned very quickly into the mainstream of Hollywood movies. I directed Breaking Training when I was twenty-six, then did some independent films and then went back and did Doctor Detroit (1983) and the Richard Pryor movie Some Kind of Hero (1982). I had a run of about six feature films over the first ten years of my career. It was really *The Great Texas Dynamite Chase* that launched it all.

SA: *The Great Texas Dynamite Chase* is one of these road films that appeared so often in the early and mid-seventies. It seems like almost all of the film was shot away from the studio. How was that with location management, shooting, set-ups and so forth?

MP: We shot it outside of Los Angeles, basically substituting San Fernando Valley for Texas. I remember doing things that I would never have done today. I mean, we drove an hour and a half to a location. I remember we shot in a town called Gorman. We'd get up at 5:30 in the morning, drive there, get there between 6:30 and 7:00, and I remember shooting in Gorman the whole scene where the Ellie-Jo character is hitchhiking and gets picked up by Claudia Jennings. And that looks, for all intents and purposes, like flatlands Texas. But we were shooting an hour and a half outside of L.A.

Everything was on location. There were no sets. They let us into the banks. I think it was on weekends. We shot in towns like Moorpark and Piru. We had scheduled the scene when the girls escape on horseback. In that final sequence, they use their car and put it in high gear, and it explodes into the police cars. We had to save it for the last day because we were going to blow up these cars. It rained for about four weeks, and we shut down and had to wait a month. It felt like a month. Maybe it was two weeks. I don't remember exactly. We got to this barn. We convinced them to let us use it. We had to save the shooting for the last shot. The people kind of went nuts on us. I don't know how we did it. I know we got a crane down there, and we used a crane shot for when they ride off on horseback.

SA: It's a beautiful shot.

MP: It was elaborate. We were elaborate. And it just went on. It was a little crazy. We were careful. No one got hurt. We had a scene where they steal a car. Do you remember? They run out of a bank, and they grab this lady's car. It was a Mustang, I think, because they were cornered. As the car in the first shot pulled out in reverse, the axles collapsed, and the car just collapsed on us. We're going, "Oh, my God. What are we going to do?" And our assistant director finds another Mustang in the neighborhood and convinces the lady to let us use it. We literally changed cars within a half hour.

I also remember we had an investor who let us use his Rolls-Royce. If you remember, there is a period of the movie where the three of them are together. They're in a white Rolls, and they go backwards down the street. Just before they hit all the garbage and the boxes, we had to cut. Then we did the shot from inside the Rolls-Royce. I remember turning to this guy and saying, "I said you're in for ten, but you're risking forty." We had an amazing team. The screenwriter was a guy named David Kirkpatrick, who ended up being president of Paramount Pictures for a while. A major executive who was a classmate at CalArts, who I'm still in touch with, Sean Daniel, was a second assistant director. He became president of Universal, and now he's got his own production company. Jamie Anderson, who shot, I think, Hollywood Boulevard and probably some other Paul Bartel movies, was a wonderful cameraman. And it goes on from there.

SA: So you have wonderful technical talent, but you also have pretty good creative talent. I mean casting talent. What I find fascinating about the movie is the interaction between the two principals. I mean you have Claudia Jennings, who's this sort of exploitation sex bomb, but it seemed like Jocelyn Jones was just able to almost pull more of the attention to herself. She has a supporting role almost, but she's so good in it.

MP: You're right. We auditioned Jocelyn. I don't remember how we met her. She and I have still remained close. I saw her a couple years ago, and she emails me, and she's become a wonderful acting teacher. She came in and read for us, and she was terrific. I remember that she treated the sex scenes, or sex scene, with complete theatrical seriousness. It was not like she felt like she was prostituting herself. In fact, she had a boyfriend who played the character in bed with her, Miles Watkins. They've been married and together ever since.

So Jocelyn's a wonderful lady, wonderful actress, and was the saving grace because Claudia Jennings—I wouldn't say she was a very stable woman. She was pretty out there. Not much of an actress, but somehow pulled it off. I think that she had serious problems. I remember we also shut down because I think she had a little bit of a nervous breakdown for a week or was on drugs or something. She was not stable. I was not shocked. I was saddened, but not shocked, when I heard that she died in a car accident. And I don't know the details. Do you? Did you ever know much about her death?

SA: Only that she was twenty-nine, and I think she crossed a traffic line.

MP: I think she fell asleep at the wheel.

SA: Yeah, right. I think she was driving to a boyfriend's house at four in the morning, and I don't know about if she was sober or not.

MP: I would guess she wasn't. God. When did she die?

SA: She died in 1979. She was twenty-nine. She's one of these people like Pam Grier or Sybil Danning who has a cult following. In *The Great Texas Dynamite Chase*, Claudia Jennings offers viewers camp, and Jocelyn Jones is so.... I don't know how to describe it. It's like there's a realism to her performance, and meanwhile people are blowing up cars and holding up banks.

MP: Jocelyn helped to root the movie. Her credibility helped, and I think you could then identify with her. Johnny Crawford was lovely in the film, too. He was very, very gung-ho, very easy to work with. He took direction well. I remember really liking him, and he was very empathetic. We developed a really good trio with them. If you remember. There was a period of the movie where the three of them are together...

SA: Yeah.

MP: And then there's a supporting cast of pretty varied types. There was Oliver Clark, who had that small part as the police officer at the beginning of the film, a brilliant comedian actor. Then we had Tom Rosqui, who played Claudia Jennings's father. He had a small role. Daniel Sullivan, too, who's the famous Broadway theater director, probably the most successful Broadway theater director today in our country. And he was a struggling actor. Priscilla Pointer's also in the movie. We pulled people left and right—terrific actors—to be in the film. The acting was one of the other great fortes of the movie.

SA: I think that's one reason why it holds. Because it fulfills the objective of being an action-adventure-comedy, but it has this compelling quality, the grace notes, if you will, that bring you back. And you're like: Look at what's on display there. Look at how this camera moves here or how this shot holds. And that's what makes it so enjoyable. I'm wondering, did you have any of Mackendrick in your head as you were making the picture? Because—

MP: Yes. Yes. I was about to say that the things that I had learned in film school having to do with framing, and staging, and honoring Mackendrick's approach both in terms of comedy and style was something that I was able to apply to this movie. I mean, it is a.... I don't know if I want to call it a satire, but it certainly is a satirical comedy. We went with that idea. And I will say honestly, David Kirkpatrick, who wrote the screenplay, was also a student of Mackendrick's. We were really dealing with a lot of the things we learned in film school. And I will say, Mackendrick was.... He was very complementary about the film, and he was a very tough teacher and a tough character to get that, but I do remember him saying he liked what we did with the movie. He wasn't crazy about the subject matter, if I remember correctly, but he thought the style was there and it showed great promise.

We put our heart and soul into it, and I had no idea what would happen, because I didn't really know what we had. We still traveled by the seat of our pants, almost with blindfold on, in the sense that I remember the very first screening of the film. There was no rough-cut screening. We just edited it, and had a two-day mix, and we screened it at a big theater at 20th Century Fox. And somehow we got four-hundred people there, and it was explosive. I had no idea what we had.

PAUL CHIHARA

Interview by Stephen B. Armstrong

STEPHEN B. ARMSTRONG: Prior to working at New World and writing the score for *Death Race 2000*, what experience did you have as a composer?

PAUL CHIHARA: Well, I had resigned from UCLA in 1971, but I had gone off on sabbatical for a couple of years, so I owed the music department a couple of quarters work. We worked it out casually that I'd come back and teach a quarter every so often, so I happened to be in residence. I wasn't really teaching, I was just visiting the department, cleaning up some things in the archive, museum, studio and so forth. And that's when the phone call came from Roger's assistant, Julie, whose last name I do not know.

SA: Julie Corman?

PC: No. That's a good question, but Julie was off doing her own pictures by then. New World came to me for this reason: in 1971, there was a picture

81

released called *A Clockwork Orange* (1971). The score is credited to Wendy [formerly Walter] Carlos, but the music was actually by Henry Purcell—his stately *Music for the Death of Queen Mary*. As Stanley Kubrick always does, he started temp tracking the film with some classical music. And supposedly Wendy adapted Purcell's compositions into electronic versions. Actually, much of that was done I was told by a man named Paul Beaver, the assistant to Robert Moog. Moog invented the Moog synthesizer, of course. He used to build Wurlitzer organs and repair them in Ithaca, New York. That's where his studio was, and, by some celestial coincidence, at that time I was a student at Cornell, which is in Ithaca. I knew about what he was doing. *Clockwork Orange* made a big impression on Hollywood because everybody knew the score was done with these little boxes—analogue boxes. They were not very expensive relative to hiring a symphony orchestra, and the sound was very, very hip. And one of the most popular LPs at the time was *Switched-On Bach*.

SA: Which Carlos arranged and performed.

PC: Yes, and it sounded like classical music, but it also sounded very contemporary. That's what Roger really wanted for *Death Race,* and he wanted somebody who could do that sort of thing. That's why his assistant called UCLA's electronic music studio thinking Roger could get a student to provide bits and beeps and stuff that were usually associated with the electronic music of that era. Anyway, I was tired of academia, and I had already resigned. I headed down Sunset Boulevard—New World Pictures used to be on Sunset Boulevard, right on the Strip, just a few miles from UCLA. And that's how I got the gig. Up until then, I was a classical contemporary composer. That meant in the late 1960s and early 1970s two things: we were a member of what we called the avant-garde, and we were anti-Vietnam. This is very important because my generation of people actually went to war. We didn't want to, but we had conscription. We were all against the war, and we were against anything that was like an establishment. That included the "university." That's one of the reasons why the music of that period is so interesting to me. It's basically irreverent music. And if it combined things that were anathema to us when we were students all the better: for example, the combining of pop and rock and roll and classical music. The great pop musicians of that time, especially George Martin, were exploring crossover compositions. There's a string quartet in the George Martin's arrangement of "Yesterday" by the Beatles, right?

SA: Right.

PC: "Eleanor Rigby" has a double-string quartet. They were doing all these wonderful records. Take Judy Collins. Her arrangements were by Josh Rifkin, who is really a well-known musicologist and a very, very good keyboard player. He created two of Judy Collins's most magical LPs—with a cornucopia of ideas, classical or baroque or folk or whatever. There were so many fabulous new sounds. That's the world that I believed in. My own music, believe it or not, was very strictly twelve-tone. That was my generation. We were all beginning to rebel against that. I had had many successful concerts at Tanglewood and in New York, and shortly after I got to Los Angeles in 1966, I was asked to become one of the four music directors of the Monday Evening Concerts, where Lawrence Morton, I'm sure you know, served as the impresario for Monday Evening Concerts, and the organization did more premieres for Igor Stravinsky than anybody else. That was my background. I was a member of the avant-garde. I was also advisor to Zubin Mehta and the L.A. Philharmonic. And then in 1971, I became the first composer-in-residence with the newly created Los Angeles Chamber Orchestra, whose music director was the then relatively unknown Neville Marriner! When I quit UCLA that year, I had no particular commercial experience whatever. There was no way you could study that at a university or at a conservatory in those days.

But I actually did have a great deal of experience as an untutored boy in pop music. I grew up in Seattle during the Second World War, and being Japanese, I was "relocated" to an internment camp from 1942 to 1945. My family lived in Block 14, and every Saturday we had movies in our mess hall, which was a sort of escape from the barbed wire fences. And at the movies what did I hear? I heard classical music. It was called "underscore," but it would have been Mendelssohn or Wagner, as well as Korngold or Max Steiner or Roy Webb, to name a few of these incredibly talented and versatile composers. I was being fed a diet of wonderful music from the Romantic era. Growing up in Minidoka relocation camp from age four to seven, I began singing in our little informal gatherings in the canteen. Without music lessons but with a very good ear, I sang songs to our assembled "captive audience"—songs such as "Blues in the Night" or "Shina No Yoru" in Japanese. Later during the Korean War, I played pop violin with my sister, Catholine, on piano in a USO troupe, entertaining our troops bound for the Far East.

When I got this opportunity to write a movie, *Death Race 2000*, I jumped at it. I realized that I had always wanted to work in Hollywood. That's why the score that you hear is such a mélange of different styles. First of all, to have a multicultural and chronologically jumbled world of music and sound had become completely acceptable for a young avant-garde composer in that era. Today, I think that concert style is referred to as "postmodern." The cinematic version of it, when it's mixed with digitally altered Foley, is known as "sound design." But, second, I didn't know any better. I had no formal training in jazz and pop music or anything, although my teacher at Tanglewood was the formidable jazz authority Gunther Schulller, who years later persuaded Mercer Ellington to bring me to Broadway me as the principal orchestrator for Duke Ellington's hit musical *Sophisticated Ladies*.

SA: Fantastic! And you're so right: the music in the dance scene in *Death Race* does seem to straddle the popular and the avant-garde at once.

PC: With respect to that dance scene with Mary Woronov, who was a big favorite of the film's director, Paul Bartel, I wanted to come up with a really bizarre kind of rock and roll, what I thought futuristic rock and roll would be. It sounded far out then, and I still like it. But young composers in film today are not intimidated by bi-tonality! When Roger hired me, they were almost through shooting. And that's why he went to get me, the electronic music effects guy. I don't know who they had in mind for composer; no one told me. I don't know if they ever did have somebody in mind. My guess is that they were just going to play with effects as opposed to an underscore. But I provided them with the score, which delighted everybody, probably because it was from a rank amateur.

SA: How was it working with Paul Bartel?

PC: Paul was a lot of fun. I saw him as a sort of lunatic genius! He didn't tell me what he wanted. But every time he heard something of mine, he just laughed, and then he'd put it where I didn't expect him to. That was his real gift. He never thought inside the box—or any box I could imagine! He reminded me of a junk-store curator—a junk-deposit junkie, like you have in certain parts of downtown L.A. or maybe way down in the Village in Manhattan—just obtaining stuff and putting it together. I thank heaven Paul was my first ever director in Hollywood. He taught me to enjoy working in the movies!

SA: As I understand it, Bartel would take your music and edit it and play it against the film in the cutting room. You must have had some communication, some commiseration.

PC: We met all the time. There was a studio on Vine Street. I'd go there every day, and I'd bring in these tapes. Everything was tape in those days. I'd record them, sometimes at UCLA, sometimes in my own home in Santa Monica. I never played the material for him beforehand. I never gave him a mock-up of the music. I'm a violinist, not a pianist, so I couldn't really demonstrate my music. I would make these tunes, and I'd bring them to him, and he'd listen to them. I never heard him say "This sucks." What he said were things like "Oh, that's good, I can put it in chase scene" or "That works in a love scene" or whatever. Then he would take the track—his film editor was his music editor, Tina Hirsch—and they would just put it up on the old Moviola and try it. They would immediately transfer my two-track tapes to 35mm tape, "four-track" as they called it then. They'd put it up on the Moviola against picture. He'd play it, and he'd say, "Isn't that working? It's good." Fortunately, I gave him good tempos. I don't know where I learned that—someone had taught me that obviously—but I sensed that the music needed to have "push." So I gave him tempos that were upbeat, and therefore he could cut anything to it, and it seemed to help. He never asked me to rewrite a thing. He just took what I gave him.

SA: Did you know him after the production, after post?

PC: I ran into him many times after that. I used to see him around here in Manhattan. I didn't work with him after that. I'd probably like to have, but I was at the beginning of my career. I think he was at the middle or toward the end of his when we worked on *Death Race*.

SA: What about other work you did for New World?

PC: I did another picture with Roger Corman called *I Never Promised You a Rose Garden* that made a star of Kathleen Quinlan. And I was part of the team of people that put together a movie that Roger bought in Tokyo called *Submersion of Japan*, one of those disaster movies that everybody was making in the 1970s. He changed the title to *Tidal Wave*, and it starred Lorne Greene, who was his friend. We all dubbed that, though none of us on the subsequent soundtrack had been trained in ADR, and I certainly am not an actor.

One thing I'll say about Roger Corman. Some might call him a cheapskate: he didn't pay us much. Well, he paid us a little bit—but I think we all lost money in doing these gigs. But he gave us full screen credit for our work. After *Death Race 2000*, I had a career. I haven't stopped working since. I owe it all to him.

LINDA SPHEERIS

Interview by Stephen B. Armstrong

STEPHEN B. ARMSTRONG: Would you mind speaking about your early interest in movies and art?

LINDA SPHEERIS: I wasn't ever really interested in art that much. In college I studied microbiology, but I sort of got tired of that. I met this production designer, Peter Jamison, and he was working for New World Pictures. My sister, Penelope, was at UCLA in the movie department, and for the master thesis, they do a movie. There was a guy named Alan Jacobson, and he had backing and enough money to hire people for his thesis film. I was hired, and I made $150 a week. I did costumes, sets. We shot all around UCLA. I was even an actor in one scene: I rose up as a dead person in a real morgue doing the slate. Alan Jacobson was killed on a motorcycle, and he never got the chance to put that movie out. It was after that I met Peter Jamison. Peter did a lot of production design for the Corman movies. When I met him, he was in his office, and there were all of these wads of paper thrown around because he was trying to design a wardrobe; I didn't know how he could do that because there was no money. He was quite creative. That's how

I started. I don't remember really what the first movie was, probably *Crazy Mama*. It might have been *Big Bad Mama* and then *Crazy Mama*. From there we did *Eat My Dust!* and *Grand Theft Auto*, which was Ronny Howard's first movie.

SA: Where did you go to school?

LS: I studied microbiology at Long Beach State, and then I left there after two-and-a-half years and went to Santa Monica College. That's when I got an interest in art. I started taking art history classes, photography, whatever I could get out of that school. I got encouraged to go into art because of my newly developed interest in movies. Then I went to UCLA and developed an interest in production design. I kind of went all over.

SA: How old were you when you started working on these films?

LS: I was in my mid-twenties. I was in one of my sister's films, about some transsexuals. Penelope had a company called Rock 'n Reel, which was before MTV. They did videos of rock and rollers, and we worked on those, going all around the country shooting artists. I didn't do anything technical at all; I just helped her move the camera. We didn't have sets, so it wasn't that big of a deal.

SA: Was Penelope working on New World Pictures films like *Crazy Mamma* and *Grand Theft Auto* with you?

LS: I was working on those without her. I'm not sure when she did *Decline of Western Civilization* (1981), but I worked on that with her. People in the mosh pits would always come to the camera, and I would have to push them away so they didn't knock it over.

SA: What else did you work on back in the 1970s?

LS: Something called *Vigilante Force*, a Gene Corman movie, in 1976. That had Kris Kristofferson, Bernadette Peters and Jan-Michael Vincent in the cast. Jack Fisk was the production designer, and Sissy Spacek was the assistant art designer. Jack is a great production designer. We worked in oil fields and had to do some interesting stuff. One time there was a small house we had to move because we wanted it in a different place. We put big four-by-fours underneath it, the whole art department at the time—there were twelve of us. We lifted it up underneath and walked it over to where it was supposed to be. I was really strong at that time in my life, so it was fun to do. These things were always very hot and very dusty: all of the locations were. We didn't have the amenities we get these days, like craft services and water. But we didn't care because we were all on drugs and alcohol; as long as we had our quotient of that it was okay.

SA: Was it weed? Or stronger?

LS: We drank beer and liquor and did speed and cocaine. I don't really remember doing pot, but it was never heroin or anything like that—mostly it was just things to keep us going. A lot of speed. That's what I remember the most. By the way, I'm now thirty-six years clean and sober. I'm not into any of that anymore. It was just sort of a time when everyone was doing it. When I first started doing union movies we would have medics, and they would come and give us B12 shots.

SA: Tell me about the learning process that came with these low-budget pictures, especially for a set decorator.

LS: We established the environments for the characters, but we also sort of did everything. First of all, there were no production meetings. We had no office space. I didn't meet with the director very often, but the production manager probably did. We tried to coordinate with the costume designer. We built, decorated and destroyed the sets. There was a prop guy, but there were no special effects, no greens, no paint department. There was a stunt department, but we made the stunt people whatever they needed; they didn't oversee their own stuff like they do now, which they should have. It always made me nervous to make ramps and pads for stunt people, but that's what we did, and we did it on a shoestring.

Our budget was a van. That's all they gave us—a van. We had to go around and find anything we needed, and that's why we called ourselves the "trash artists." We would just pull anything we needed out of the trash. Mattresses were easy to find and old chairs. Most of the time, if we didn't shoot in a place that was all ready as is, we were going to drive a car through it, we built these fake parts of a house and stuffed wadded-up newspaper in the walls so that when the car went through there was more stuff to come out. We had to paint the wood so it didn't look like it was new once the car hit it. One time we had a fish tank that they had to go through. One time I had to rig a frog in a salad bowl. People were supposed to walk by, and the frog would jump up. There was a bunch of lettuce on top of him. It was a real frog, and we had a stick taped to him. I was under the table, and I would poke the frog up when people went by. The frog peed, and there was all this pee coming out of the hole in the salad bowl. That wasn't very fun.

One stuntman got killed. We didn't make the ramp. I don't remember what movie that was on, but the jump was by a parking structure. After that I was always very cautious about anything we had to do to facilitate stunts. There were no cranes. There were a lot of things that would give people a heart attack if they had to do them now. These days OSHA has given us these guidelines that we have to safety-pass. We have to take classes all the time; they include everything from sexual harassment to operating a lift. There was none of that stuff, even in union movies, back then. We were very versatile; we sort of did everything that they needed.

How that impacted me was that I got hired a lot. When they would look at my resume, they would go, "Oh, wow, she knows how to work with no money!" That was really a plus. Then it got to be sort of a minus because the movies were so bad. But for the most part it really helped. I used to get violations all the time when I first got into the union because I would do the same things I had done on Corman movies; if I would move a tree, if I moved greens, if I tried to rig an effect, the union would cite me. All of these things we used to do we couldn't do anymore.

SA: What was the payroll situation like for those low-budget non-union movies in the 1970s?

LS: I don't really remember. I don't know if they gave us checks. I can't remember. You can bet I got paid every week, or I wouldn't have been there.

SA: But you liked the work? You enjoyed it?

LS: It was so exciting. Being around making movies was fascinating. I mean I got to work with Mr. Magoo [Jim Backus, on *Crazy Mama*]. It was just really fun. Of course, it was so abusive, too. I mean, looking back on it, there were times when I was up on the roof installing some neons, and I fell off the roof because I was so tired and drugged. It was scary: what we had to do, what they expected. There were twelve-hour days and longer. We had to be there before everybody else to get the sets ready and then stay after to clean the sets up. We were there at least twelve hours a day, most of the time eighteen, and then we had to drive home. We couldn't have done it without speed, or I couldn't have at least, and I'm pretty strong. On an administrative level it was very loose. There were no production meetings. No script readthroughs. We didn't even break down the scripts. We just followed the order of the production designers. There was all the prep work that we never really had any prep for. I'm sure we had a shooting schedule, but it wasn't clear about the direction we were taking. It could have been, too, that I was on drugs, so I don't remember. But I do know that we didn't have production offices or meetings.

SA: You often hear about how quick these low-budget shoots were, but it seems like efficiency could be lost if there wasn't a great deal of leadership at the level between the production manager and the team. How was it that you guys were on point, on target, with your activities when it was such a scramble?

LS: The production designer kept tabs on what we had to do. Back then, I didn't know how to break down a script. I didn't know how to create for a character. I tried and became sort of like a method decorator; I just sort of became the character and created what they would want. Did you know that Billy Paxton was part of our team? He was one of the "trash artists." He left pretty quickly, but he was really good at bringing things in that would go with the character.

SA: Did you interact with casts much?

LS: We would always have to move things around for them, but I wasn't associated with the casts that much. I always thought it was a proper thing not to bother them. That's sort of been my whole career, in fact. I have very few pictures of actors that I've worked with. The ones that I really liked I got. But I just don't bother them. It's sort of an unwritten rule: you're hands off and you don't interface with them. They're focused on other things.

SA: I guess that would be the same with the Cormans? You were the laborers and the management was elsewhere, right?

LS: I remember very little exchange with those guys. I remember one time we were in Griffith Park, and there was an ambulance, and it came to pick up Julie Corman because she was having her baby. I don't even remember most of those people. I remember Teri Schwartz a little bit. It's just a big fog. It's probably something I choose not to remember.

SA: Did you get the sense that young people like you who had talent were being exploited?

LS: I definitely think that that's the case. On the other hand, it was the School of Hard Knocks. A lifetime of use came with the knowledge I got from those movies. I can tell the people who started in the union, and I can tell the ones who have done a lot of independent stuff. You really have to want to bleed for the production if you love movies. And we did. They were exploiting us, but we were also getting an education that you couldn't have gotten anywhere else. There was a fifty-star flag one time—I think it was when we were shooting *Vigilante Force*—and it was up on a flag pole. They said, "Oh, my God, that's the wrong flag; we have to get the forty-eight star one." I put the correct flag in my back pocket and shimmied up the pole, and I released the one, and then I hooked the other one up. I think that if people won't do stuff like that, they're not going to be good workers later on. They really have to be team players, and producers know that, too. They can tell who grew up in the union—and the ones who are good at improvising and probably can keep on budget. Yeah, we were being exploited, but I think at the time I made about $300 a week. I went from waitressing to that. It was fine. I was happy.

When you're young and you have the knowledge that this is my path, and you have the passion for it, that's worth so much. Being there, getting experience, getting excited, knowing that I created something: that creative urge really got satisfied. That's probably the biggest thing that I got from it. The other side of being exploited is that you know when not to get exploited in the future because you've been through it in the past. Working on these films forced me into drugs and alcohol, which was instrumental in helping me to get off drugs and alcohol later. It was instrumental in getting me hired on a lot of jobs because of having to improvise and keep on budget. A lot of people put a lot of worth into Roger Corman movies because they know that they did a lot with a little. That's the goal of a lot of producers today.

It's a totally different business now, and I'm really grateful that I was in it when I was. We were more like a family then. We moved from movie to movie, and we pretty much all stuck together. Roger Corman knew who he could get and what their worth was. That bond that we made was really everlasting. I mean I haven't seen Bill Paxton in forty years, and this last December I saw him at a party. He grabbed me and kissed me and was so glad to see me, and it was so good to see him. We all really had this affinity. When Peter Jamison died, it was a part of me that died, too. He was Pappy, we called him Pappy. It was an extended family. For all of us who grew up in war-torn-battlefield families, which I'm sure a lot of people like me did, it was such a relief to find a new place where we could just feel connected, feel loved and get our creative urge satisfied. I didn't even know I had a creative urge, and now I feel like that's the purpose of mankind.

LEWIS TEAGUE

Interview by Robert Powell

ROBERT POWELL: How did you first meet Roger Corman?

LEWIS TEAGUE: I met Roger through Martin Scorsese. I had gone to NYU with Marty, and he had done a film for Roger called *Boxcar Bertha*. Roger called him after that, asking him to edit another film. At the time, Martin was working on *Mean Streets* and could not do it but referred Corman to me. Roger called me to see if I was available for editing. I think that was about 1972. I was co-directing a low-budget film called *Dirty O'Neill* (1974) and wasn't available at the time. But a few years later I was trying to figure out how I could get the opportunity to direct a film. I decided to cultivate a relationship with Roger. I heard that an acquaintance of mine, Monte Hellman, was about to direct *Cockfighter* for him, so I called Monte and asked if I could edit the film. Monte said if it's okay with Roger it's okay with him. I called Roger and told him that Monte would like me to edit. Roger said that if it was okay with Monte, it was okay with him. That is how my relationship with Roger started.

RP: What was Corman's initial filmmaking influence on you?

LT: I knew that he had directed a bunch of films for American International—the Edgar Allan Poe films with Vincent Price. I cannot say that he had an aesthetic influence on me. I admired him as a producer, but not the films themselves. I saw him as a very smart person who had a great eye for talent and could get talented people to work below their normal pay grade for the credit opportunity. The impression was confirmed when I first met him and began working with him. I really liked the way he dealt with people. He respected creative people; he set the parameters very carefully. And once he hired somebody, he let the person work under those parameters with a tremendous amount of freedom and support.

RP: Describe working for Corman.

LT: As I said, he set the parameters very clearly. I began working with him as an editor. Monte Hellman edited the dramatic scenes in *Cockfighter*; I edited the action scenes. I edited four or five films for Roger altogether and then began directing second unit. He was very specific about what he wanted. When we edited something and screened it for Roger, he would always watch with a notepad, scribbling notes and turning pages. When the film finished, he would say "Let's go back to my office." We would go back to his office where he would say "We've got a film in there somewhere." Before giving us the notes, he would say "I only expect you to address about 85 percent of these notes. The other 15 percent will probably address problems that you've already tried to correct." He would then give specific notes and never talked about problems without giving one or two possible solutions. I really liked that. Then he would let us go back to the editing room and make changes. About a week or two later, we would have another screening. He was smart and so clear and knew exactly what he wanted in terms of a film. His primary concern was that the films be commercial. He once said, "Lewis, I will never lose money on a film if I have the right title and budget." I directed second unit on several films for him, and then directed my first feature *The Lady in Red,* for him. He gave a script written by John Sayles, who had just won the MacArthur "Genius" award. He asked if I wanted to direct it. I said, "Absolutely." I loved it. His restrictions were that I had to work within a $450-thousand budget. He said that I had to shoot it within twenty-two days and work with a specific group of actors that he requested to help with selling the film. Beyond that, he let me cast it any way that I wanted. He was on the set the first day of shooting, and after that, he let me alone until I delivered the director's cut. Then he came to the first screening and took notes just as he did when I was an editor. It was a delight to work with him because you knew exactly where you stood. We did butt heads a couple of times. I had a different opinion about a scene he asked me to cut. I said I really thought it should stay in. There was a pause. He then said, "This is the producer talking to you. Please cut that scene out." I said, "Oh, okay."

RP: Tell me a little about your experience with Corman when you were adding new footage to *Cockfighter.*

LT: Roger wanted to amplify the action at the end of the film. Monte was out of town, so Roger gave me a very small crew for a day that included stuntmen and chickens. I went out and shot some more cockfighting footage for additional sequences that I cut into the film after the end. Those shots amplified the sequence but didn't make a qualitative difference at all. They were not that important in the long run. Roger had given Monte a lot of freedom. *Cockfighter* was different from most Corman films. He usually made genre films, such as student and nurse or women-in-prison films. These allowed for titillating scenes and action. *Cockfighter* did not fit into any of those genres. And the story was challenging because it was about a cockfighter who had taken a vow of silence until he could win the coveted "Cockfighter of the Year" award. The main actor, Warren Oates, was walking through the film silently for most of the movie. It had no sex or car chases.

Roger thought since cockfighting was popular in the South that Southerners who liked cockfighting would flock to the theater to see the movie. He was wrong. It opened and flopped; nobody came to see the film on its opening weekend. I was in the editing room when Roger came in and said, "Lewis, I was wrong. I want to change the trailer for the film. I want you to take all the shots of sex and violence that you have and give them to Joe Dante." Joe was doing trailers at the time. I told Roger that Monte didn't shoot any sex scenes or violence. Then Roger said, "I don't care where you get them, just get them." I had to go through all these old films—student and nurse films and car-chase films—and pull out a bunch of shots that I gave to Joe Dante that included action and sex. This didn't seem ethical to me. I called Roger to tell him that it didn't seem right to me to put scenes in the trailer that are not in the movie. Roger thought about it for a second, and he said, "Lewis, you are right. Put these scenes in the movie." I had to go back and figure out a way to add all these irrelevant shots into the movie. I created a dream sequence where Warren Oates falls asleep and dreams about cars careening around corners and nurses exposing their boobs, and then he wakes up. I thought that was hilarious.

RP: In *How I Made a Hundred Movies in Hollywood*, Corman says of *Cockfighter*: "To my knowledge, no one had ever made a picture about cockfighting. Now I know why. No one wants to see a picture about cockfighting. The picture failed. I thought it was an interesting, commercial film about the dark side of rural America. What can I say? I was wrong." What would you say about Corman's willingness to take chances, his ability to admit his shortcomings?

LT: It really stems from his intelligence. He is just such a smart guy. If he made a mistake, he would have to be truthful about it. I don't think he made many mistakes. He erred on both of the grounds of budget and title in *Cockfighter*. I think he spent more on *Cockfighter* than on his other films. He was relying on the name *Cockfighter* to market to people interested in that sport. He was smart enough to make a correction of this error. I don't think Roger was motivated by ego. He was very self-effacing. This is a key reason why he could admit where he was wrong.

RP: What did you yourself learn from Corman's efforts to save *Cockfighter*?

LT: Roger's desire to make money was what kept him working on that film. None of those things improved it. The upside is that Roger's desire to make money would enable him to keep churning out low-budget films and continue hiring new people. He wanted to encourage talent, but his primary reason for doing that was that he could get them to work for virtually nothing. He was smart enough to find people in the film business desperate for an opportunity and pay them virtually nothing. He could make films on a low budget and make a profit at it. He was very successful at that. And he gave a lot of talented people their start.

RP: Joe Dante has referred to *Cockfighter* as a bizarre movie that was really more of an art film. What do you think of this assessment?

LT: I agree with that 100 percent. Monte is a filmmaker with a very unique and great personal vision. Monte executed his vision on directing the film. That makes it a kind of bizarre film for Roger to have made. *Cockfighter* did not fit into any of Roger's genres at that time. It was an art film, I guess, in the sense that it was a film made by a cult filmmaker who executed his own personal vision. Monte was the director and primary editor. I was co-editor and directed the fight scenes exactly as Monte wanted. I don't think the film had excessive violence. As unpleasant as it may be for people to watch cocks fighting with each other, it was primarily a dramatic story. I was executing Monte's vision. I accepted that it was Monte's film.

RP: Do you think the non-speaking aspect of Warren Oates's role was more or less difficult than a typical speaking role?

LT: I believe that it is more difficult for an actor to enact a role where he's got to communicate what he's feeling nonverbally. In *The Revenant* (2015), I had tremendous respect for Leonardo DiCaprio's ability to play that character without the crutch of dialogue. That is why he won the Academy Award. The same is true with Warren Oates. Not having dialogue made his job much more difficult. Kudos to Warren Oates for accepting the part and doing such a good job with it.

RP: Arguably *Cockfighter* is a cult classic because no film like it was made before it and probably never will again.

LT: The film deserves a lot of credit, and Roger deserves a lot of credit for making it even though he erred in its commerciality. He recognized that Monte was a very talented and unique filmmaker and gave him a great opportunity. Even though his primary motivation was to make money, Roger also wants to be recognized for the incredible opportunities that he gave to dozens of filmmakers, from me to Joe Dante, Francis Ford Coppola to Martin Scorsese and so on. *Cockfighter* is a little gem of personal filmmaking. It had so much integrity. Monte and Warren had a vision of a certain kind of film, and they executed that vision and fulfilled his personal filmmaking desire. I think that *Cockfighter* should occupy an important spot in the pantheon of Roger's filmmaking, revealing as it does his willingness to invest in talent. If he hadn't been running a commercial enterprise and did not make a little bit of money on all those films, he would not have had a chance to give so many directors an opportunity and a toehold in the industry. Many filmmakers made good films for Roger their first time around; *The Lady in Red* is one of those. It was a success, and I am proud of what I did with it.

RP: The original version of *Cockfighter* cuts short some of the excessively brutal depictions of cocks being killed.

LT: When we were editing the film, I was extremely aware of the fact that audiences really don't like to watch animal-on-animal violence. It is more difficult for people to suspend their disbelief when they are watching two animals fighting than when they are watching two human beings fighting. They are aware that there are more protections in a fight scene between two human beings. They are aware that these are stuntmen, who are not really hurting, shooting or killing each other. In the case of the cockfighting, the chickens were actually tearing each other apart. It is a very difficult thing for audiences to watch; they do not want to see animal-on-animal violence. Being aware of that, I was trying to cut the scenes as much as possible to show the action of the chickens fighting and the ferocity of the activity, without showing or focusing on the blood, pain and injury.

RP: Anything else you might add about your relationship with Corman?

LT: I learned a lot of very useful management skills from Roger Corman that stood me in good stead later when I began directing. Roger was very inspiring to work with as a producer and as a leader. He gave the creative people who worked for him very specific parameters and instructions but encouraged them to do very creative work. I learned from Roger the importance of working quickly. I also learned from him the ability to act quickly on my feet, to recognize problems and quickly fix them. I learned not to be locked into ego or rigid points of view. He was a great inspiration in many, many ways. I will always be grateful to him for giving me my very first opportunities: first as an editor, then as a second unit director and then as a director. I've had a very successful career, directing twenty films. This may never have happened if I had not met Roger Corman and had a chance to work for him, with him and learn from him.

JOHN SAYLES

Interview by Stephen Armstrong

STEPHEN B. ARMSTRONG: How did you end up working with Roger Corman?

JOHN SAYLES: I always liked movies. I certainly saw more movies and TV shows than I ever read books when I was growing up. But I didn't know anybody in the movie business; I didn't know how you got into it. Not until I was in college did I understand that movies were made by directors, writers and movie producers. I had gotten out of college in 1972 with a degree in psychology and started working in factories and hospitals. Eventually I got a job as a meat packer. And while I was doing that, I was writing short stories and sending them off to magazines. Around 1974 I wrote a short story, and Atlantic/Little, Brown asked me to turn it into a novel. I turned it into a novel, and they agreed to publish it. That was the first book that I got published, which was *Pride of the Bimbos*, when I was twenty-five. I started working on another novel, and what was clear, as I was also acting and directing in a summer stock company up in New Hampshire, was that although I hadn't had an agent for my first novel it probably would be a good idea to have an agent try and sell my new book while I was off acting.

So without meeting him, I got an agent through some friends that played poker with a guy named John Sterling, who later became an editor and was very important in the publishing business. My second novel eventually came out in 1977, *Union Dues*. John said, "Well, I'm going to sell this for you, but you understand that my agency has a deal with a second agency in California, and automatically your novel is going to be represented and could be made into a movie." I didn't think it would be made into a movie, nobody ever bid on it, but what I said was "Can I have that contact information for the film agency on the West Coast?" I got in touch with the second agency, Zeigler, Hellman & Ross, and they said, "Well, great. You want to come out and be a screenwriter? Send us something." I had just read Eliot Asinof's book *Eight Men Out* at the time and thought it would make a very good movie. without owning the rights or knowing how to get them or anything like that; I just adapted that and sent it out to the Zeigler agency. It turned out Evarts Ziegler, the head of the company, had been Eliot Asinof's literary agent twenty-five years earlier when he had written the book. And Ziegler basically said, "Look, there is a curse on this thing, and it will never get made into a movie, but you did a good job adapting it. Come on out here, and we will see what we can do for you."

My partner, Maggie Renzi, and I moved to Santa Barbara in about late 1977, and I was assigned to an agent named Maggie Field. She took me around, and let me meet people at the bigger studios. One day, she called me up and said, "There is a rewrite available at New World Pictures for a movie called *Piranha*. If you want it, you've got it." From what I understood later, Frances Doel had read a couple of my short stories that had been in *The Atlantic* and passed one on to Roger, and he said, "You know, let's see if we can hire this guy." I drove down to Brentwood and had a meeting and was given this screenplay to rewrite, which was *Piranha*. They weren't crazy about the screenplay, but they loved the title. They loved the idea of making a spin-off of *Jaws* (1975), which had been very, very successful. I did one draft before I even got to talk to Joe Dante, the director. He had been editing for Roger. As I remember, I wrote two-and-a-half drafts of the screenplay, and we changed it quite a bit. The final draft was just stuff for Joe once I got to meet him that was more in line with his budget, which was under a million dollars.

SA: My understanding is that in the draft that you were working on there was a bear chasing people, and there was a fire chasing the bear...

JS: Yeah, they were kind of hung up on how to get people into the water, and as I remember some woman had menstrual... *you* know. And she went into the water and was eaten. At another point, there was a bunch of hippies around a campfire, and the bear chased them in the water and then the piranhas ate them. I felt like if piranhas are hungry, they don't need blood to be in the water. It's not like sharks that are only attracted to blood; if they are hungry, they are going to eat whatever they bump into. I just felt like once somebody knows there are piranhas in the water, there has to be a reason for them to go in it. We were going to have characters whom we follow for a long time, I had to come up with a reason for them to travel in the water in something that is not very substantial. I thought immediately, "Well, what if they have to take a raft down the river to warn people that there are piranhas in the river?" That seemed like there was more of a chance for them to have central characters who are in constant danger rather than "Oh, we have to go back in the water again. I wonder if they are still in there."

SA: You received guidance from Frances Doel and Roger Corman for these changes or followed your own instincts?

JS: Their might have been notes from them about adjusting the pacing and giving the audience some relief if there had been a lot of attacking, but I knew about adjusting the periods of intensity in the story from all the creature features I had watched growing up. I was a fan of them. They usually had some giant monster, a giant whatever. There was a giant grasshopper movie called *Beginning of the End* (1957). *The Day of the Triffids* (1962). *The Blob* (1958). Plus Japanese ones like *Mothra* (1961) and *Godzilla* (1954). Generally, in these movies there is a manifestation of "The Creature." *Creature of the Black Lagoon* (1954) was the first one I saw fairly often. I felt like "Ok, if you're going to make an eighty-five minute movie, you should probably have six or seven attacks before the final big one." Some kind of manifestation, even if it doesn't pay off. So the audience knows "Don't stick your foot in the water." And the central character gets away without getting eaten, but there is some suspense to it.

SA: You had the plot worked out for *Piranha* and from there you built your characters?

JS: They kind of go together. You say: "Who is going to have to go down the river in a raft? Well, who is up the river where there are no roads? Who is a recluse?" That lead me to the idea of somebody who had a drinking problem and was a bit of a hermit or a curmudgeon. And this thing kind of lands in his lap, and the only way down the river because he is in a remote place is to get in a raft. Then you have somebody who knows about the creature, who is an ichthyologist or a mermyecologist, so you throw that in. And then the bad guys kind of come out of the question "Who would put such a thing in the water if it doesn't happen naturally?" I had been aware of a bunch of shady things the American government had done: like testing nuclear weapons and using LSD and not telling their own soldiers that they were in the test and not doing a very good job of dealing with their health problems later. I felt like this could be one of those Agent Orange things, where the government goes a little too far with its testing and they don't want to admit it; they want to hush it up. Very often the plot demands the characters.

SA: What you started addressing and anticipating was another question I had and that was the theme the social message of the piece, the social criticism, the anti-militarism of it. That just emerged from the storytelling? Roger and Julie Corman are pretty emphatic about being political radicals.

JS: It's their discomfort with authority, which includes the police and the military and the government. Authority in general. These are movies that mostly teenagers were watching, and teenagers love movies where authority is questioned. If you go back to *Rebel Without a Cause* (1955) you know the adults in that movie are no bargain. In the era that I was writing in, people were really questioning the government especially because of the Vietnam War. You see that in a lot of the movies that the Cormans made, there is this basis of questioning authority.

SA: You had a part in *Piranha*. You were one of the soldiers.

JS: Yeah, it was like a cameo. Part of it was that they needed a few little touch-up rewrites, and they were shooting down in Aquarena Springs, which was not, at the time, a very new resort. As I remember, there was a drought in California when we first got there that lasted a good five, six years, like the most recent one. The rivers didn't have enough water in them to support a lot of shots of a raft going down, so the production ended up in Aquarena Springs, which is kind of between Austin and San Antonio. In the movie, because it was a spinoff of *Jaws*, there was the cloned idea that a new resort was going to open and the greedy owners didn't want people to know that they were going to be in danger because they were going to lose money and the resort could not open on time. Obviously, the equipment in Aquarena Springs was not new. I wrote a couple lines for Dick Miller about recycling things. But it was also fun for me to come down and be on a movie set; I had never been on a movie set before.

SA: *Piranha* was a pretty big commercial success. That must have pleased Roger. You were eventually brought on to do a film that Julie Corman produced, *The Lady in Red*.

JS: I didn't really work with Julie that much because I only did two-and-a-half drafts of it. Roger had made *The Valentine's Day Massacre* (1967) film, and he had made a couple other gangster films. It was a genre he was trying to revive because *Bonnie and Clyde* (1967) had been so popular. He just handed me this idea of writing something about "the Lady in Red," something about Dillinger and the woman who was with him when he got shot. I felt like I knew quite a bit about that era. I was big fan of *The Untouchables* TV show when I grew up and knew gangster lore that way that British people knew the succession of kings. I could get into all the social stuff that was happening in Chicago at the same time, the Red Scare and all of that stuff.

I was interested in this main character, this woman who is just making the best of a bad situation, who didn't set out to be in a gang that robs banks and ends up doing it because she is poor, not very educated, and she ends up in Chicago, where one in every three women under fifty and over eighteen was a prostitute. Prohibition and the Depression were going on at same time. She is kind of a victim who turns around and becomes a victimizer. Once again, there is a pretty big anti-authoritarian thing because the cops in the movie and in Chicago at the time were so corrupt that you couldn't have a whole lot of respect for them. I just ran off with that, and my first draft must have been about one-hundred-and-twenty pages. Roger and Frances's reaction to it was: "This might not be that affordable to make. Maybe you could cut it down a little."

The last draft I did, I talked to the director, Lewis Teague, on the phone, and he explained to me that he had less than a million dollars to make this epic. There was no way that he could shoot everything that I had written. Because I cut it down quite a bit after that, I did not meet with Julie during the scripting. I imagine that she was working with Lewis on the budgeting. Once the screenwriters hand the script in, they're pretty much out of the loop.

That was one that I just handed in and wished Lewis good luck. I am not sure that I even met him until we worked on *Alligator* (1980) together.

SA: Here's one thing, a quote I found recently from Julie that she gave to someone named Mollie Gregory. She says that one of things that she hoped for from you and the writing of the script was an examination of "social issues, feminism, communism, racism, The Haves versus The Have Nots. There's that fine line between hitting the issues too hard and losing the audience or just glancing over issues haphazardly. Sayles handled the balance brilliantly, and he really built people in the film."

JS: I'm not sure that I had that conversation with Julie, but that was the kind of notes that I was getting from Roger and Frances. Their concerns were never about the content, which they liked. Their concerns were with the length and the expense. It was a New World movie, and I had written something that was truly like a big studio epic. So it was more like "Okay, can we keep all this stuff. but condense it, condense it, condense it." I think it was something that Lewis liked, as well. It made it more interesting than the average gangster picture.

SA: One of the points of the film that stands out for me is the whole sweatshop encounter. How does that tie into your own experience, if at all, with your work in packing plants?

JS: It was basically something that I had always been aware of. I grew up in Schenectady, New York, which was a big General Electric town, and they were always battling with the Electricians' Union over contracts. But having worked in both union and non-union jobs was something that I really understood: where unions came from, why they were necessary and what situations were like when there weren't unions. That sweatshop era, which was still going on in New York, Boston and various other places where I had lived, and that potential for exploitation were something that I wanted to get into the movie. Why are people desperate? Why are they willing to become bootleggers? Why are they robbing banks? Some of it was poverty, and some of it was even if you can get a job, it's not a job that is going to make you enough to live comfortably at all. You are working for slave wages and lucky to get them. That system was maintained by the police. That was a connection that I wanted to make clear: that the FBI and the police were automatically anti-union because their true constituency was not the American people; it was the people who own those factories, who had good connections with a politician. In most cases, they were directly paying off the law and people who protected their interests. It was something that I was glad that stayed in a somewhat reduced way in the movie. The character that Pamela Sue Martin plays goes through these stages, this innocent agricultural background, then to the city, and she runs up against the hard edge of the city quickly. For unmarried, unemployed women, there weren't too many avenues to make a living, and she tries a couple of the legitimate ones and doesn't do well. So she ends up being a prostitute.

SA: I keep recognizing how these movies that came out of New World have parallels with the situations that we find ourselves in right now. Just the other day I saw something in the newspaper about how it is virtually impossible now in the United States for a minimum wage worker to make rent on a one-bedroom apartment.

JS: There is a great book that I actually adapted that Showtime never did as a series, although they developed it for production, called *Nickel and Dimed* by Barbara Ehrenreich. It was written maybe ten years ago, and she went out and tried to survive on minimum wage jobs. She worked at a Denny's, she worked at a cleaning service, and she worked at Walmart and she couldn't do it. Even going to the food bank, she was failing to make a living. She discovered things like the pretty woman with the nice dress who was the hostess at Denny's was sleeping in the parking lot because she couldn't afford an apartment. She was happy because Denny's kept the lights on, and there was security all night. She had a friend who worked at a motel nearby, and that is where she went to change her clothes and take showers while the woman was cleaning rooms. It's not as bad as it was in the 1930s, but stuff still goes on, and human nature is human nature.

One of the things that I think was fun working for Roger was that as long as you really paid attention to the genre beats, to the rhythms of the genre, to the satisfactions of the genre, he was actually very happy to have it be about more, to have it be a more interesting movie, to have the characters have some depth. He could get better actors interested sometimes, he could get more interesting directors, and that gave the movies more impact.

BELINDA BALASKI

Interview by Stephen B. Armstrong

STEPHEN B. ARMSTRONG: How'd you get started in movies and TV?

BELINDA BALASKI: I was a child who heard a voice in the hallway. When I was five years old, I was walking down the hall by myself, and I heard this big voice, and I, being raised Catholic, was sure it was God. Who else could it be speaking from the hallway? This voice said that I was going to be an actress and my life was going to be about communication. I remember saying "Okay," and I walked on. Everything I did from that point on was based on that moment, including shortly thereafter organizing all the kids in the neighborhood, writing plays and charging the parents a nickel to come.

It was the beginning of everything. I had drama scholarships from seventh grade through twelfth grade in a private girls school, then again in college. And when I got here to Los Angeles, I did have some luck, as I was cast in a play called *Bus Stop,* at the newly formed Met Theatre. I

113

did three William Inge plays. The first being *Bus Stop*, the second *The Dark at the Top of the Stairs* and the third was *Picnic*. *Bus Stop* was directed by Jim Gammon with Tim Scott and a bunch of guys who had just done *Macon County Line* (1974). When *Bus Stop* opened at the Met—it was a forty-seven-seat theater—everybody on the planet came. We were sold out for the entire five weeks we were running. It was the first year L.A. put the small theaters up against the large theaters in awards. We walked out with Best Play, Best Director, Best Supporting Actress, which was me, Best Supporting Actor, which was Fred Downs, and Best Set. This was over the Ahmanson Theatre, the Mark Taper Forum, the Dorothy Chandler Pavilion, the Shubert, everything here in Los Angeles. This teeny tiny theater walked out with everything. From that point on, all the people came, all the producers came. Robert Duvall was sitting in the audience. Cloris Leachman. Robert De Niro. It was such a tiny theater you could almost see everybody. Having done all three Inge plays and winning Robbys for the other two, I became very visible. A lot of people came to see me, and suddenly I was working.

SA: Where did you go to college?

BB: I went to Colorado Women's College, and I did not graduate. I graduated high school in 1965. I was sixteen when I went to college. Most people are eighteen. This is because I was five when I started first grade. I don't know how that happened, but, anyway, I just skipped everything. I'm pretty smart. I was sixteen years old in college, around 1965 or 1966, I guess, when the whole world changed, and I was on the cutting edge. Basically I was expelled from college, and ended up in Iowa taking classes at Parsons College but not really enrolled, yet very involved in the college theater and the town of Fairfield. I ended up getting married and coming back to the Northern California area and then slowly but surely making my way back down to L.A. because I wanted to be an actress.

That was in November 1970 when I finally arrived here, and I was very committed to doing what I had to do to make it. I was always so driven. It was the next year or the following that I was cast in *Bus Stop* and everything just sort of happened step by step. You get connected to the right workshop, meet the right people, the right agent. My agent happened to be Jim Gammon's agent. It's funny how this whole business works—or used to work—I'm not so sure it does anymore.

As I said, I ended up winning the L.A. Drama Critics award for *Bus Stop*. Then two Robby awards: one for *Dark at the Top of the Stairs* and again for *Picnic*. I had done *F.B.I.* and *The Cowboys*, with Bobby Carradine, by the way, and ended up in an audition with Jack Arnold, who was doing a Fred Williamson pilot called *Black Eye*. I was supposed to be one of these evangelical converts, where you get touched on the forehead and you sort of melt into a delirium and then convert. I had seen this in a documentary years before called *Marjoe* (1972) about Marjoe Gortner. Many years before that, before I came to L.A., I lived in Half Moon Bay, south of San Francisco. There was this house in the area that everybody avoided because Marjoe's mother lived there. There were all these stories about the terrible things she had done to her son in order for him to learn his sermons. We always just gave the evil eye to the house. We were terribly afraid of this woman that we never saw, and now here I was in L.A.; and when I had this audition, I thought, "Oh, my gosh, I better use *Marjoe* as research. I rented the movie, and I watched people fall into delirium for two hours at a time. I watched it five times in a row and went in and auditioned for Jack Arnold. I did it once and he goes, "Can you do that again?" "But of course," I said. And I did it again, and sure enough I got the part. And there I was on set with Jack Arnold, and his daughter, Susie Arnold, who was also acting in it. Susie ended up in casting and eventually cast *Piranha*, but by then she and I had become really great friends.

So the years passed. I did *Locusts* up in Canada with Ronny Howard and Ben Johnson. I did "Runaways" for a Hanna-Barbera *Afterschool Special* as the runaway, a character named Cindy, and it won the Emmy that year. Then suddenly I'm in this workshop with Merrie Lynn Ross. Peggy Stewart was in it also, who had played my mother in *Picnic*. The director Mark

Lester, who was going with Merrie Lynn, came to see everybody at one of our workshop showcases because she'd said, "Boy, if you want to cast your movie, everybody's great in our workshop." I was doing the part of Laura in *The Glass Menagerie*, and he ended up casting me as Essie in *Bobbie Jo and the Outlaw* (1976). When I went to meet Lynda Carter, I realized, "Oh, my gosh. She's so beautiful. She has this amazing body." I was so aghast by her beauty that I called Mark up, and I said, "Look, two beautiful girls are never friends. It's always the opposite. Can I go with beveled glasses and dye my hair red and gain thirty pounds?" Mark said, "Okay, you can do the glasses, you can do the red hair, but you may not gain a pound. Okay?"

The interesting thing about *Bobby Jo* is that Tina Hirsch was editing, and Mark had no place for her to edit. So Tina went to Roger Corman and asked Roger, "Would it be okay to use an editing bay at New World?" And he said, "Of course, help yourself." Tina ended up sitting next to this guy she didn't know, who was putting together his movie called *Hollywood Boulevard*. They introduced themselves: "Hi, I'm Tina Hirsch." "Hi, I'm Joe Dante." And when they would do their cuts, they would go: "Hey, what do you think of this?" "Hey, what do you think of that?"

Now I never knew any of this until years later. But that's how Joe "met me," watching Tina edit *Bobby Jo*. How I ended up being in *Cannonball!* came directly out of *Bobby Jo* and another AIP picture, *The Food of the Gods* (1976). I was sort of in that eighteen-year-old category, even though I was actually nearly thirty-something playing eighteen. I was going from film to film. So I auditioned for Paul Bartel, and he cast me in this part as Maryann in *Cannonball!* And I had a great time on that.

It must have been two years after *Cannonball!*—yes, it was 1978—when Susie was casting *Piranha*. I went in for this interview, and here's this little guy, Joe Dante, who says, "Hi, we've worked together before." As I'm walking across the room to say "hello," the room just lengthened about ten feet. I was thinking, "What picture have we done together? Oh, my God! Who is this?" And as I approached him all of a sudden, I said, "You're that greasy little mechanic in *Cannonball!* You were wonderful!" And he said, "You

116

remembered me!" And from that point on we were just great fans of each other. Was *Piranha* New World?

SA: Yes.

BB: Was *Cannonball!* New World?

SA: *Cannonball!* was partly funded by New World. Paul Bartel had had a falling out with Roger Corman while he was making *Death Race 2000*— another movie Tina Hirsch edited.

BB: I didn't know that.

SA: An associate of Corman, Sam Gelfman, had tried to secure financing from Fox for *Cannonball!*, but then the money fell out, and he went to Roger, who said, "Yes, I'll put some money into this. I'll invest in this." The picture had help from New World, but it wasn't actually a New World production.

BB: Was it just independent then? That's the way I remember it. *Bobby Jo* is AIP, right?

SA: Yeah. I keep thinking about these connections between movies and people. *Macon County Line* was an early film Tina Hirsch edited.

BB: *Macon County Line* was one of my original auditions in this town. The director was Richard Compton. I had three callbacks for that part, and Cheryl Waters got it. Now while they were in Georgia making *Macon County Line*, there was Jim Gammon and Timothy Scott, there were the Vint brothers—Alan and Jesse—and Max Baer. Here they all were on set. "Look, we got some money," they were saying. "Why don't we go back to L.A.? We'll open ourselves a little theater, and we'll do some plays." "What plays? What plays are you talking about?" "I don't know. We could do *Bus Stop*." Jim

117

loved Inge and all that old country stuff. "Who will play what?" "Well, Alan you can play Beau. And, Timmy Scott, you can play Virgil. Max, you can play the bus driver." And that's the way it happened.

One step led to the other. There was once a heartbeat and a soul here in L.A. Now that heartbeat is all CGI or something. It's gone. Everyone was in there 'kicking it' in the day. You look at a movie like *Bobby Jo and the Outlaw*. There's Jim Gammon, Jesse Vint, Virgil Frye, Peggy Steward, Gerrit Graham. Look at *Cannonball!* There's Bill McKinney, Veronica Hamel, Gerrit Graham, the Carradines. So many brilliant actors in these movies. An eclectic group of young director guys came out of film school together, Joe, Paul, Jonathan Kaplan, George Lucas, Brian DePalma, Steven Spielberg.... And they loved each other, and they used each other in each other's films. Joe is in Paul's movies. Paul is in Joe's movies. Rogers in everybody's movies. They loved to do that. They're film buffs. That's what they do best.

SA: Allan Arkush was telling me that for the people working at New World back then the religion was film. And everybody was a priest.

BB: Everybody was a priest or a convert or just a person who went to the same 'church.' Because this was our religion. And we did nothing else. We breathed, ate, lived film and theater. That's all I ever did. Film and theater, film and theater, theater and film. When I went to college, I was supposed to take all these other classes. I never even showed up for them. I wasn't going there for that. I was going to do theater. In fact, when I was in ninth grade, I begged my mother to take me to Pasadena Playhouse because that's where I wanted to go to college. She drives me up to Pasadena Playhouse, and there was Steve Allen doing this whole lecture. Everything in the room stopped, and all I could see in there was him.

Of course, years later, there I was in *Amazon Women on the Moon* (1987) roasting him at my husband's funeral, which is so funny. It's a moment he didn't understand, but it was full circle for me. I did not apply to a single college because I was going to Pasadena Playhouse. Yet guess what happened halfway through my senior year.? Pasadena Playhouse closed. How did that happen? Did God not want me to act? My whole plan just went kaput. At that point I started applying, trying to find colleges last minute. Colorado Women's College accepted me on a full drama scholarship, which I'd been on for seven years in private schools. So that's where I went. It's just really funny how this life thing works.

SA: Let's go back to *Piranha*. In one of the DVD extras I remember you mentioning being in a screening room, and Roger said something about "More blood!"

BB: The scene where they tied the piranhas to me—they actually put gaffer tape on my skin. This was Rob Bottin and Jules Roman. I know Joe likes to say Rob was eighteen years old, but I swear he was sixteen when I met him. I can see him sitting across the pool with his head in his hands, thinking about how he's going to do this. They literally put gaffer tape on my skin and fishing wire that tied the rubber fish to me, and then they helped me carry twenty fish to the pool, and I got in. The problem was that after putting the Karo syrup for blood and everything into the pool, they shot too wide. You could tell they were the only fish in the pool. Roger wanted two things: more blood and shoot it tighter. This was a good thing, actually, because at that time when Jon Davison approached me about a reshoot, I said, "Oh, okay. On condition that I can get the billing I've wanted, which is star billing. And can I get a bodysuit?" We both laughed for a long time. I got the billing and a bodysuit. They put the gaffer tape on the bodysuit.

SA: I need to ask you to clarify something. The pool at USC was where they dumped all the Karo syrup. But I thought that the tape stuck to your skin because of the heat in San Marcos, that the sun had been blazing on you. I presumed that that must have happened in Texas.

BB: No. We were underwater in the pool for a long time. Joe doesn't like

119

water, and so being underwater was not comfortable for him. It was difficult because everybody had to duck underwater. I'm a fish—I don't care—I could do this all day. It was not an issue for me. The problem was they just shot it too wide. That's all.

SA: So the business with you with the tape and they're peeling it off of your skin and it's hurting and everything—that was in L.A.? That wasn't in San Marcos?

BB: Yes, that is at the pool in L.A. The stuff where you see me in the inner tube reaching for her, Melody Thomas Scott, that's in San Marcos. But where you see me literally being dragged away or going under, that's in the pool. They've got all these crew guys, every one of them, all on one end of the pool. They had a rope around my feet. They had Joe and the camera at the other end. Those guys yanked me from one end of the pool to the other. That's the shot where it looks like I'm going down. But I'm really being dragged just under the water to the other end of the pool. It's a great, effective shot, as I've heard from many people. Unfortunately, I know what's happening.

SA: Your character, Betsy, she's so likeable you want her to carry on.

BB: That's so nice. Well, this is what John Sayles said—he wrote *Piranha*—and when we were shooting *The Howling* (1981), during the morgue scene, he said, "I wrote this part for you." I said, "What part?" He said, "Terry Fisher." I said, "What?" "After watching you, what you did with the part of Betsy in *Piranha*, I fell so in love with that character I had to take her and write her in *The Howling*." "Oh, my gosh!" "There was no Terry Fisher in the book. I made her up. Actually, you made her up." That's quite a compliment.

SA: In *Piranha*, you have the introductory shot with Betsy being kind to the little girl, and there's that business of them throwing darts at Paul's face. It's almost surprising that there's actually not a lot screen time for Betsy in the film. She's one of the more memorable characters because we develop such affection for her.

BB: Thank you! And yes, you have those moments that draw you into her. The other thing is that in John Sayles's script there is no scene between Paul Bartel and me. But here we are, both Paul and I, in San Marcos going: "God, Joe, here we are on set, and we don't have a scene together." Joe is looking at us like "Okay, okay." And we go: "We're just here, and we don't even have a scene together." And Joe just says, "Could you leave me alone? I'm trying to shoot." "But, gosh, Joe, we'd really like to have a scene together. After all, we are both here." Finally, he said, "Go write one!" I said, "Okay." So that night I wrote the midnight scene when Melody Thomas and I are sitting on the edge of the water, and we get ready to take our clothes off for a midnight swim. And Michael Katz, who had been the lighting guy on three films prior for me gave me this big full moon. It was so great. These guys were great. We shot that scene, and I think it's a real turning point in the film. It's that moment where you go "Whooaaaa, what's happening?" I don't think it would be the same film without that scene. But that's what's so wonderful about working with Joe. He gives you that room to create. He'll listen to you. He's just a real guy. If you could turn his head into a computer and do a printout, you'd have about seventy books pour out of him. He's got so much information in there.

SA: These movies with you that came out of the Corman factory, what do you ultimately think?

BB: I feel like I was very fortunate. Not only meeting Joe and being able to do twelve films with him. I sort of just landed in a situation that most people don't really find themselves in in Hollywood. And I feel so blessed to be in the Roger Corman "family." I have to say Roger is the seed of a million careers, mine included. Without Roger, half of those people that I worked with would not have been working. From Jack Nicholson to everybody-you-can-think-of started through Roger's doors. He's such a magician, allowing everyone to fulfill their creative dreams and trusting all this fresh talent. He's always loved fresh talent. I just feel fortunate because I don't know how anyone becomes an actor now.

SA: If Roger recognized talent, he just sort of let the people go, making it so a lot of these films have individual personalities. They're strange and they're beautiful at the same time.

BB: They have that Paul Bartel signature or that Joe Dante signature or that Allan Arkush thing—I mean it's very clear that there was a lot of improv going on, a lot of freedom allowed. It was such a brilliant group of guys that came out of film school together, and we were all so very lucky.

MARK GOLDBLATT

Interview by Stephen B. Armstrong

STEPHEN B. ARMSTRONG: What led you to the movies?

MARK GOLDBLATT: I was a film nut from the word "go." I don't know how it was that I became one of these people, but I couldn't see enough of them. I grew up in Brooklyn, New York. I would see a lot of movies, a lot of science fiction and horror, Saturday matinees. I was able to see big Hollywood movies by directors I would later come to understand were called *auteurs*. For example, I saw *Rio Bravo* with my dad in 1959 during its first run, its first weekend, on the big screen in Brooklyn. With people like Hawks and Hitchcock and Ford, I could tell their films were stylistically different from others'. A Hawks film felt like a Hawks film. When I was eleven, I got my first movie camera and went around and started making movies. I started collecting movies by other people. I was collecting 8 millimeter, so they were silent versions of sound films, but it was just great. I couldn't get enough. Then I got my first feature films: *Nosferatu* (1922); a cut-down version of *Battleship Potemkin* (1925), with the step sequence; *The Cabinet of Dr. Caligari* (1920). I used to screen these movies in high school—I ran a cinema club, the first time they ever had one at our school.

So I was pretty well-versed in film. Self-educated. Growing up in the New York area, we had several TV stations that ran different film packages all week long: *Million Dollar Movie*; RKO films on channel 9; Allied Artists on channel 13; Warner Brothers on channel 5. I was saturated. By the time I went to college I knew so much about film that I disdained taking the film department classes because they were so rudimentary. In fact, some of the course instructors used to borrow my prints to run in their classes.

SA: Which institution was this?

MG: The University of Wisconsin, which at the time had a fledgling film department. It was based on the concept of film departments growing out of English departments, always about narrative cinema. I was very snobbish. I did become the film critic on the daily newspaper, though, and ran one of the most prestigious film societies on the campus—the Union Film Committee—in a small 35mm screening room. In fact, the projector and the whole projection booth had been built with a grant from Fredric March, an alumnus of the University of Wisconsin—there was a little plaque there for him. At the film society, we would try to show films that would blow people's minds and often films people didn't know about, which we thought they should know about. I guess that would translate into "cult cinema."

For example, I had caught *Once Upon a Time in the West* in 1969 at its first opening in Madison, at a drive-in theater, the Big Sky Drive-in, I think it was. The film blew my mind. As a committee we talked, and we decided to book the picture for our Play Circle theater, which was a small thirty-five-seater. By the time it came to us, though, they had cut fifteen or twenty minutes, which they edited out of the print, and they didn't do a very good job. You could see Lionel Stander's barroom scene, but there were just twenty-four frames in it left. Of course, *Once Upon a Time in the West* was screened in bastardized condition for years until it was pretty much restored as much as possible in the 1970s. There was *Night of the Living Dead* (1968), too, that I saw first run at the drive-in. We booked it in our screening room, and before the weekend

124

was out it was a new cult phenomenon: kids would go to see the movie and dress up as zombies, eating turkey parts and chicken drumsticks, as the next audience was waiting in line.

I went back to New York when I graduated. Bummed around. Lived at the Chelsea Hotel. Saw a lot of movies. Realized I'd never be happy unless I tried to work in the motion picture business. I saw an ad in *Sight & Sound* magazine one day for the London Film School, where they had great teachers who were professional moviemakers. The English film industry was somewhat depleted in those days, so they hired a lot of good people to teach because they weren't making as many movies in England anymore. MGM's facility at Borehamwood had closed down. Hard times for the British film industry.

So I went to London. I learned everything. I learned how to take a Mitchell camera apart and put it together. I learned about story. One of my teachers was Mike Leigh. Val Guest and Clive Donner were two great English directors who were also teachers. Val Guest had directed *The Quatermass Xperiment* (1955). Great directors, great training. My editing teacher was Frank Clarke, who'd edited *Blowup* (1966) for Antonioni. I was inspired and realized I had a talent in that area. My plan was to graduate, leave the school for a while, maybe teach, save my money. Then go back to the United States, make my way to Hollywood, California, and try to get a job in editing. I eventually did that. It was a slow, hard slog trying to get my foot in the door. I worked on some industrial films and managed to make a living, kind of-sort of.

I was living in Hollywood, and one day I went to the movies. There was a theater called the World Theater on *Hollywood Boulevard* near Vine Street. They had triple features. Toplining the triple feature that day was *Death Race 2000*, directed by Paul Bartel for Roger Corman's New World Pictures. I knew Roger's films. I had been a big fan of the Poe movies, the science fiction and horror films, the motorcycle films, even the Film Group films. I had seen a lot of them... *Little Shop of Horrors, Bucket of Blood*. But for the New World thing, Roger was producing, and other people were directing. The films kind of had a raw energy to them.

Death Race 2000 inspired me very much. It was edited by Tina Hirsch,

125

who later became a colleague. When I saw the film, I was blown away. It just pushed me to go right into Roger Corman's offices determined to land some sort of job, and that's what I did. I went to New World and saw the secretary, and I said, "Whom do I talk to about a job in editing?" "Well, you could talk to that guy over there." And that guy over there was Jon Davison. Jon Davison was the head of production at New World Pictures and also head of advertising.

Jon was about to produce his first movie, *Hollywood Boulevard*. It would have a $50-thousand budget. Ten days for shooting using stock footage from other Roger Corman productions. Joe Dante and Allan Arkush would co-direct. Jon offered me a job as a PA, no pay. I took the opportunity and ran with it. I was very happy to be given this position—working eighteen-hour days. It was a great experience, and I got to bond well with Joe and Allan and Jon. It was their first picture, too, really—we were all in it together. From that I was hired for another PA job, this time for $150 a week. I was moving up in the world.

Jon and Joe and Allan were all film buffs. Film collectors. I was talking to Jon the first time, we discovered that we shared a love for an eclectic variety of movies. We could talk about Hitchcock, Truffaut, Goddard, Jean Renoir, Georges Franju, Roberto Rosselini, Mario Bava, Dario Argento. We were open to all genres. We were also heavily, all of us, into the *fantastique*: science fiction, horror, Charlie Chan mysteries, westerns, lots of eclectic stuff. Even when we were done working on that movie *Hollywood Boulevard*, we would get together on weekends and run movies from our collections, or we'd borrow prints from other people's collections. Great times. Great movies.

Working with all of those individuals helped my career as an editor. One of my first big jobs—certainly one of my most cherished—was working as a kind of an assistant editor to Joe Dante. I think the first time we did that was on *I Never Promised You a Rose Garden*. Joe came in to edit some reshoots. I became his assistant/co-editor—an associate editor. From that, Joe went on to edit a movie called *Grand Theft Auto*, with Ron Howard directing in his debut, and Joe hired me to be first assistant/co-editor again. I actually got to

126

cut. That was great. He kept bringing me back. When he got *Piranha*, he hired me as his co-editor. *The Howling*, as well.

These little films we were doing like *Piranha* and *The Howling*—because they were directed by someone as masterful as Joe and because we had the luxury of great scripts by John Sayles on both of them—these pictures were pretty damn good for what they were. They all made a real impression, and they made money at the box office. Joe's star was ascending. Spielberg saw *Piranha* and *The Howling* and was impressed. He gave Joe a picture. At first, I think, Joe did a little segment in *Twilight Zone: The Movie* (1983) and then *Gremlins*. I think that's the correct order. By then, Tina Hirsch was doing major motion pictures. She came back, took over the editing chores, and I went off on my own in my own direction as an editor.

SA: Your career soon took a really big turn at that point, right?

MG: Gale Anne Hurd, at the end of the New World days, was producing for Roger. She'd been his personal assistant for a long time. Gale saw what I had done on *Humanoids from the Deep*, which was a picture directed by Barbara Peeters. On that film we had a lot of production problems and issues. I did the best that I could, and the picture went on to become very successful for Roger and New World Pictures. When I was cutting a difficult scene for *Humanoids*, Jim Cameron, whom I had only vaguely met when he was working on *Battle Beyond the Stars*, was standing in the doorway, watching me work. Between Gale's recommendations to Jim and Jim's observations, they hired me to do the *Terminator* in 1984. Actually, that picture got delayed. It was supposed to start in 1983, but Dino De Laurentiis preempted Arnold Schwarzenegger's calendar. Arnold, that is, had a previous commitment with the Dino De Laurentiis Company for *Red Sonja* (1985). So *The Terminator* was put on hold.

But eventually Gale and Jim made it, and for me it was a great experience, a terrific creative experience. Everything worked. *The Terminator* edited itself. I just did the manual work. Sometimes, the way you do a movie in the editing room you allow yourself to surrender to the material, submerge yourself in the material and manipulate the material to a point where the material is editing itself. You're just a spirit medium in the universe. I know that sounds a little airy-fairy, but some of my best work has resulted that way, a product of semi-conscious editing. The success of *The Terminator* (1984) enabled me to go on to bigger Hollywood studio films. I did a couple more films with Jim— *Terminator 2* (1991) and *True Lies* (1994). I got involved with Joel Silver and did *Commando* (1985). Prior to that I had done *Rambo: First Blood Part II* (1982) with George Cosmatos. Later on, I went with Michael Bay and Jerry Bruckheimer. I had a career that blossomed. None of this would have happened, I'm convinced, if I hadn't walked into the offices of New World Pictures that fateful day.

DURINDA WOOD

Interview by William Nesbitt

WILLIAM NESBITT: Tell me how you started working in movies and television.

DURINDA WOOD: At the end of high school and in college, I worked in summer theater in the costume department. Summer theater gives you an incredible boot camp experience for anything in theatrical arts. I went to Bard College in New York and went through their fine arts program. Then I got a BFA in design from CalArts in Los Angeles and after that attended the design master's program from Yale University's School of Drama. I met many colleagues along the way that brought me into theater, film and television.

WN: How did you find you way to *Battle Beyond the Stars*, and what role did you play in the production?

DW: In those days, Hollywood was much smaller, so information circulated freely and quickly through small groups and friends. I heard about *Battle Beyond the Stars* through word of mouth, and some friends who knew my work recommended me as costume designer. After a brief interview, they had me make some drawings of possible costume designs for the movie over the weekend. I think I was competing with several other people. This was highly unusual to have to design the show before you got the job, but I was hungry since I had only designed one other film. I was thrilled I got the job. I spent several nights drafting designs nonstop over the course of a single weekend, and they obviously liked what I did. The rest is history. In addition to the limited time I had to get everything together, this was also the first time I had to think of designing in terms of science fiction, and I wasn't really into sci-fi before *Battle Beyond the Stars*—kind of ironic given all the work I would later do on *Star Trek*—so that added to my trepidation. I was exhausted at the end, but the good news was that I didn't have to do as much work for the movie once I was hired because I had done so much work upfront. My early designs laid much of the foundation for the finished costumes.

WN: What recollections do you have about making *Battle Beyond the Stars* and of Roger Corman?

DW: It was very fast-paced, and there was a lot of work to be done in a short amount of time with very, very little money. I came into contact with Roger only a few times on the shoot, as he seemed to give the cast and crew a wide berth, I had the impression he was working on several things at once: fingers in many pots, so to speak. My impression was that he was running a little studio on a shoestring, and the pressure was to make a silk purse out of a sow's ear. He was a tough negotiator, I think.

WN: How much direction was there?

DW: From Roger, not a lot. I just went through my notes from that time. I received three comments from Roger on the costumes. The main group of aliens needed to be a little more modernistic. The character Dako needed to be more serious and scarier. And St. Exmin, the Valkyrie, needed to be sexier.

He understood he was working in the B movie genre, and he asked for what he thought would sell tickets. Changes were made, and all were approved.

WN: Describe the pace of working on *Battle Beyond the Stars.*

DW: It was very, very fast. There were four weeks of preproduction and then eight actual weeks of filming for a big sci-fi movie. I worked nights, weekends, eighteen-hour days. Grueling. Relentless. It was film boot camp. I had only a few people in my crew. But we made it. We were all still young and didn't know any better.

WN: Corman is always very conscious and protective of a film's budget. Do you have any examples of that?

DW: I was paid $650 a week and had a budget of $25 thousand that would have been like a million dollars or more for a film like that today. I had two assistants. I went back to my theater roots and had everything built at the Center Theatre Group shop. The quality of the work was fantastic, and the expense was far less than a Hollywood film costume shop. It all worked fantastically well because of the professionalism of the theater artists that I hired, and it stretched a miniscule budget. I was designing very fast and by instinct. For example, the Kelvin communicated through heat, and I wanted their costumes to reflect that. Reflection literally became the key to the whole thing. I located a material called Scotchlite that is very reflective. Safety people, night workers, people building highways—they all wear it, mostly as vests. Once I outfitted the Kelvin costumes with Scotchlite, I worked closely with the cameraman, who could adjust the light mounted on the camera up or down, and it would simulate them getting colder or hotter. Little things like that were fairly cheap, but the value was in the innovation. That's the sort of thing I really learned how to do because I had to do it all the time for that film. The experience helped raise my costuming to the next level, and it helped me learn to trust my instincts. That is what was required for a Corman film.

Another time I went to a place that sold building materials, bought some nylon screening, added some nuts and bolts and things like that, and created the costume for Cayman. One must be resourceful. And while there were aliens and lizard-men and so on, it all had to maintain a certain level of believability and consistency within the world of *Battle Beyond the Stars*. That could be difficult with the limited funds and narrow timeframes we were allotted.

WN: Did you interact with any of the actors or film crew?

DW: Of course. That's the job of a costume designer. I developed the characters with the actors, made adjustments, made sure things were fitting properly. A lot of the casting wasn't finished until the last minute, so I was bumping up against those tight timeframes, as well. John Saxon, who played Sador, the main villain, wasn't cast until four days before he needed to be filmed. That's tough to work with. I really like to see the actors and their bodies in person before I design for them. I want them to feel comfortable, and I need to get a sense of not just who they are but who they think their characters are and how the actors plan to play their characters. I had envisioned Sador as a less elegant character than how Saxon envisioned him and what he became. So I took someone I saw as more of a thick brute and made him more elevated, more regal. I had to turn him from sloppy into smart, crude and rude into refined and royal—polished. In fact, Sador's original costume was going to be the costume I designed for the rougher, brutish Malmori that he rules. Later, I used the same material that I used for Sador's costume for the music group Devo.

WN: What did you learn from working on *Battle Beyond the Stars?*

DW: This was an early film for me, so it was a time of tremendous growth. I was working with Jimmy Murakami, John Sayles and Jim Cameron, some real talent. I learned a lot more about the day-to-day workings of a film set.

132

I learned to think and work on the fly. For example, the heads of the Nestor weren't right the day before they were to shoot. We didn't have time to ask the prosthetic crew to redo them, so we improvised, using foam and hoods. It still didn't come out quite how I wanted, but well enough. That's the downside of working on a low budget. However, the various departments worked together really well and helped bring out the best in each other, so I learned the importance and strength of teamwork, not just with the members of a team but with getting other teams, other crews to work with, to communicate with and to help each other.

WN: Any unexpected challenges?

DW: All the rain caused a lot of problems. Halls and sets were flooded in the warehouse in Venice that Roger chose to shoot in. Characters had to slosh themselves and their costumes through muddy water. And, of course, everybody's feet were soaked, which was incredibly uncomfortable. People say it never rains in southern California. Well, believe me, it sure did while we were shooting *Battle Beyond the Stars*. As we moved through, I would see ways to improve things. The hairstyles of the Akira, for example, were something I wanted to change, but we were too deep into filming, and changing them would have upset the continuity already established in the previous shooting. There were many challenges on that film. Too many to name here.

WN: How did *Battle Beyond the Stars* influence your subsequent career?

DW: Everything I learned I put into future films. I don't think I would have been hired on *Star Trek: The Next Generation* if I hadn't worked on *Battle Beyond the Stars* and had that sci-fi experience. I learned to work quickly and make changes just as quickly. I definitely learned more about managing and maximizing a budget.

WN: How did you think *Battle Beyond the Stars* would end up doing in the box office?

DW: I had no idea, really. It's so hard to anticipate that when you put your heart and

soul into something. You are so close to it; you have no idea if it's good or not. And it has everything to do with advertising, as well. I'm sure Roger was going to advertise it well because I think he had spent more money on it than most of his other projects. I can't remember how it did.

WN: The return was something like ten-to-one, making it one of New World's biggest hits. What did you think *Battle Beyond the Stars* would do for your own career?

DW: I thought it would help further my experience, credentials, contacts and possibilities in the film industry. I made a lot of friends that I am touch with to this day like Paul Elliott [camera operator], Jim Dultz [props] and Timaree McCormick [costume supervisor]. All of them I worked with after *Battle Beyond the Stars*. I knew that if I could have success in a Corman film, bigger things might be ahead fr me. I was nominated for a Saturn award, and I'm sure that didn't go unnoticed by prospective employers.

WN: What did you think critics would think of *Battle Beyond the Stars?*

DW: I had no idea. But it was nominated for five Saturn awards, so I guess we did something right.

WN: I know that Sybil Danning also won a Saturn award for her performance as St. Exmin. Do you think the film has a message?

DW: Yes, the message is hope. If people can come together and fight against tyranny, there is hope for a quality life. Of course, it was based on the famous Kurosawa film *Seven Samurai.* I am a huge Kurosawa fan, so I appreciated the basis for the film.

WN: *Battle Beyond the Stars* was the only Corman film you worked on. Why?

DW: Well, the pay, for one thing. I was asked to design the next film, but I wanted more money for budget and salary after I realized the amount of work involved in working on a Corman film. Roger was just not going to increase budget or salary. Also, I had other offers to work on films at the time. Some of the portrayals of women, especially St. Exmin's character, bothered me. I didn't like the sexism and the attitudes toward women in the B movie genre. They didn't match my principles.

WN: When you look back at the film, what do you think of your own work?

DW: I haven't gone back and looked at it. I think I have a copy on tape somewhere. It was a while after the filming was completed that I saw the finished product. I thought the costumes were fantastic for the money we had. I'm happy with our contribution. Since we've been talking about it, I want to see the film again.

WN: While there are plenty of examples of folks who started on small projects and then went on to much larger achievements, Corman seems to have had an incredible ability for spotting and selecting that kind of developing talent.

DW: I think Roger hired good directors and producers, and they, in turn, hired good people to work under them. Some of it may be luck. Some of it may be that because he was involved with so many films, the odds dictate that a certain amount of raw talent will appear and go on to larger projects and bigger successes, just as there are others who didn't move forward in the film industry. I think people knew that working with Corman and being successful would help propel them into other projects. Working on a Corman film was an experience, an education you couldn't get in a conventional classroom. It was a good experience. Tough at times, but good. Very practical. New World Pictures attracted young, hungry talent that was willing to work hard, work fast and, to some extent, trade pay for experience that would allow them to move up in the film business. Corman is his own film school. I think Corman films acted as a much-needed boot camp for the film industry in those days. Graduate from there—and the sky might be the limit.

WN: What is the Corman aesthetic?

DW: Does he have one? I don't know if he has a single, specific aesthetic. He made literary films like the Poe films. He made foreign films. He made more arty films. He made comic films. He made horror and science fiction. He made a variety of B movies and exploitation films. If anything, the commonality might be "Do it fast and do it cheap." Like everyone else, he does not exist in a vacuum. He picked up and used ideas that were already out there. *The Magnificent Seven* and *Seven Samurai* were influences. Those are stories well worth being retold, and he did it on a shoestring.

WN: Why do you think people like the New World Pictures films so much? Why do they continue to resonate?

DW: Do they continue to resonate? I guess they must. I haven't watched many of them, but he has been making movies this long and surviving, so he is doing something right. He is his own man and makes what he wants. That is an amazing feat in Hollywood. He's the master of the budget flick. He did a lot with a little, made purses with sow's ears, transformed lead into gold. He excelled at that and helped show others how to do it. He has educated generations of Hollywood film workers and given them a platform to be creative. I think that is his great contribution to Hollywood.

SID HAIG

Interview by William Nesbitt

WILLIAM NESBITT: How did you get started working in movies and television?

SID HAIG: This goes way back, okay? When I was a kid, I was growing so fast that I could trip over a dime. And so it was decided by my parents that I would take dance classes. I thought, "Okay." So I went, and I loved it, and I thought it was the greatest thing in the world. By the time I was seven I was being paid to dance, and by the age of nine my parents were tired of me beating the hell out of their pots and pans, so they bought me a used drum set, and I started working on that. I went through the whole music business, signed a contract with Keen Records one year out of high school, and I was selling records like crazy to radio and other places.

Nonetheless, I wasn't making any money, so at the age of nineteen I decided this wasn't working. A friend of mine suggested I look into the Pasadena Playhouse. I found out this is a great theater arts college. That seemed cool. I sent away for the information, filled out the application, got my letters of recommendation and started two years of acting boot camp. At the end of two years I graduated, and a month later I got a call from one of my former instructors saying that Jack Hill, who was at UCLA at the time, was looking for someone to play the male lead in a student film. I went and interviewed with Jack, and we got on well. I was hired for a film called "The Host" (1960). After graduation things just started happening one right after the other.

WN: What are the films that you have done with Roger Corman?

SH: Oh, my God, I can't name them all. I've done at least a dozen films with Roger Corman. He might have been directing, executive producer, writer or connected to the film in some other way, but I would say it was at least a dozen films. Some of them include *Blood Bath, Pit Stop, Coffy, The Big Doll House, The Big Bird Cage, The Woman Hunt* (1972), *Galaxy of Terror,* and *Wizards of the Lost Kingdom II* (1989).

WN: How did you get your first role with Corman?

SH: I got my first role through Roger Corman, not with Roger Corman. I did my first role because of Jack Hill. He was directing *Blood Bath*, which Roger was producing. Jack hired me for the role, and that's when I first met Roger. Nice guy right off the bat. He wasn't standoffish. He wasn't the guy behind the oak desk; he wasn't that kind of person.

WN: What is your favorite Corman film?

SH: Wow. My favorite Corman film that I did? Well, I have two. *Coffy.* And *Galaxy of Terror*, except for a couple of little bumps in the road, but it was cool.

WN: What is your least favorite Corman film?

SH: I'm hard-pressed. I guess maybe just because of production value and stuff like that *Blood Bath*.

WN: Please discuss your fifty-year relationship with Roger Corman.

SH: We've always had a good relationship with one another. Very friendly. Very honest. Very healthy. He's done a lot to help me over the years. At one point the Screen Actors Guild went on strike to get a percentage of VHS sales. We were on strike for three months. To show the kind of guy that Roger Corman is, he was the only one who sent me residuals for VHS sales. That's the kind of guy he is. I do have to add that Jack Hill was another person who sent residuals for VHS sales. Those were the only two.

WN: How did you get the part of Quuhod in *Galaxy of Terror?*

SH: Roger wanted me to play the role. He and I both have this kind of relationship where he sends me a script and a contract. I read the script. If I want to do it, I sign the contract. Then we're off and running. If there's something that just doesn't feel right, I just don't sign the contract, and there's no hard feelings, and we move on, which is a great way to do business with someone, you know?

WN: One condition you made for playing Quuhod was that you had to "to do it mute." In the DVD extras for *Galaxy of Terror*, you said that "the dialogue just doesn't match what the character should be." Can you elaborate?

SH: I was playing the old warrior, and the dialogue just didn't fit that mold at all. It was very contemporary, if you will. It just didn't seem right at all. I talked to Roger, and I said, "I'd like to do it mute." And he asked, "Why would you want do it mute?" I said, "Well, have you read that script?" And he says, "Oh, okay. You can do it mute."

WN: You said the director forced you to say the single line "I live and I die by the crystals." What was so important about that line?

SH: Nothing. It was just something that he had in his head that he wanted me to say. And I said, "I made a deal with Roger that I would do this mute." He says, "I don't care; you have to say this line." Being old school there's two rules about working with directors. Rule number one: the director is always right. Rule number two: if the director is ever wrong, refer to rule number one. So I said the line.

WN: Your co-star Robert Englund said there were times you rallied and cheered up the cast when things weren't going quite right and got a little weird. Can you give some examples of that?

SH: I don't remember exactly what I did. I just have a very positive attitude when I'm working. I try not to let things rattle me in that process. So if something was going wrong—we were working too many hours or somebody was stressed or something wasn't what it was promised to be—I just passed it off, made a joke about it, tried to kind of defuse the situation and get everybody's head back to where we were supposed to be.

WN: What did you learn from being in *Galaxy of Terror?*

SH: I learned to speak up when I asked Roger to let me do it mute. Instead of just going "Oh, okay." The lines didn't fit the character, and going along with the script when I knew that wasn't the best choice… I stood up for what I thought was the right thing. And it worked out. I learned to speak up when I asked Roger to let me do it mute instead of just going "Oh, okay" and going along with it anyway. I knew the lines didn't fit the character. I knew that wasn't the best choice. I stood up for what I thought was the right thing, and it worked out.

WN: That's kind of ironic: speaking up about being able to remain silent.

SH: Yeah, there's times when you just have to shut up.

WN: That's always a good lesson to learn, too, I suppose.

SH: Yeah.

WN: Any connections among any of the other characters that you portrayed, whether it was for Corman films or other projects?

SH: No, because I work internally. Everything comes from within, so to imitate something that I did before would be out of line with myself and my way of working. I try to make everything different unless I'm playing the same character in a sequel or something along that line. I try to make every character different from any of the other characters that I've played. All my characters are standalones and freshly created. All of my characters are unique. That special chemistry I have when I work with Roger Corman inspires me so much creatively. He's a visionary, who always brings out my best in each and every role.

WN: What do you think the thematic focal point of *Galaxy of Terror* is or should be?

SH: The fact that the things that we are most afraid of can kill us. Watch the movie and you will see this idea come up again and again. For instance, Erin Moran, Alluma, who is claustrophobic, she died with cables, cords, tentacles or whatever those were, wrapped around her body and head and squeezing her like a hot dog. Other people had other fears and their deaths were connected to them in some way. I had a fear of losing my crystals. What happened? That's the way I died. The crystals killed me.

WN: My next question was doing to be "Does *Galaxy of Terror* have a message?" But do you think that is the message, that the things we fear ultimately can or will kill us if we give them power over us?

SH: Absolutely. Absolutely. There's two big real killers. None of them have anything to do with germs. That's fear and guilt.

WN: What do you fear most?

SH: Not being able to create.

WN: What do you think Roger Corman fears most?

SH: Not being able to create.

WN: What do you see as Corman's goal for moviemaking, the common themes… his approach, his signature as an artist, his strategy for filmmaking?

SH: First thing, I don't think Roger has ever lost a penny on a film. The guy knows how to make things work. He makes them as entertaining as possible with the amount of money that he has to work with. He finances his own films, so he's only got one boss—that's him. He treats people well. Everyone that I know who has worked with him enjoyed working with him. He has certain formulas that he uses, and they work. One thing I like to joke about is that all the films we did in the Philippines have a common formula: nine naked women and me. So there you go.

WN: Why do people like the New World films so much? Why do they continue to resonate?

SH: There's just kind of a comfort to them. You know you're going to watch something that's going to be fun or silly or suspenseful or really dramatic. It's the thing that just keeps people coming back to him. He's a marketing genius.

WN: Please finish this sentence. "Roger Corman is…."

SH: Roger Corman is the guy that I will work with any time.

GRACE ZABRISKIE

Interview by William Nesbitt

WILLIAM NESBITT: Let's begin with some background about yourself. How did you get started working in movies and television?

GRACE ZABRISKIE: Dear God in heaven, I just can't get interested in that question.

WN: Did you read for the part of Captain Trantor in *Galaxy of Terror*? How long did it last? What was that meeting like?

GZ: Yes, I did. What I remember is that I had a very dear friend who was also my writing partner at the time, Carol Caldwell. She decided that she would get me up for that audition. She dressed me in a way that I knew was absolutely inappropriate for the role. She's one of the brightest women that I know, and she knew more than a little bit about the business. I understand better now why she was right because of some other experiences since. This audition was a big deal for me because I had only really just gotten to L.A. I knew I went in looking way too sexy for the role, but according to some of the comments from some other people, which I was reminded of watching the extras on the DVD reissue, it was absolutely the right thing to do in terms of getting some attention. Who was it that said something about "She looks so sexy and she had this long hair, and she wasn't wearing a bra?"

WN: Robert Englund said that.

GZ: I thought, "Well, yeah, interesting." To me that's an interesting story, and maybe to other actors who might be more of my general mind, which is to go into an audition with that actual character in mind. You don't go in overly sexualized, for God's sake. Give them a chance to see you as the character. I've had a couple of other experiences that confirm the sad truth, which is it never hurts to go in for the audition not necessarily looking like what you're going to look like in the final version of the production. Some of those stories are as close as I get to a #MeToo story.

WN Was it always clear in your mind and everyone else's that you would play the part of Captain Trantor?

GZ: No idea. I didn't read for anything but Captain Trantor.

WN: What recollections do you have about making *Galaxy of Terror* and of Roger Corman?

GZ: I think my main recollection of the shooting was that it was my first experience with "gang" shooting. It's a very stressful way to shoot from the actor's point of view. As you know, the normal way is you start a little scene, like my first scene, say, when I walk onto the ship, introduce myself and throw my weight around. So we shoot a master of that, and then we come in for close-ups, the camera keeps moving, and the lighting keeps changing for each little setup. It takes a lot longer. What they did because of time and money is shoot everything in one direction that would take place in that location. that means I go through pretty much all four scenes in the cockpit from one direction. It meant that the person I was talking to would have to remember the way I said something hours ago when he was finally being filmed responding—and vice versa. It was insane. Listening is one of the most important things you can do as an actor. Listening means you are responding to what the person said and the way he or she said it. With this style of shooting there is no way for the actors to listen and respond to each other. There's a critical dynamic that is lost.

WN: So there was a sense of trying to complete the film as quickly as possible?

GZ: Uh, *yeah.*

WN: By the time of the film's release, you had about three years under your belt in movies and television and went on to perform in many other films and shows. How does *Galaxy of Terror* parallel or detour from those experiences?

GZ: *Galaxy of Terror* was a bit of a trial by fire. I think that experience led me to really appreciate other ways of filming.

WN: That's very diplomatically put.

GZ: And true. I hadn't done that many films. For all I knew, I was in for a lot more of that. As it turns out, no, I wasn't in for a lot more of that. Subsequent films felt easier, more compatible with what seemed to me to be a way that respected actors and what actors had to contribute. On the other hand, it's not as if I felt that my contributions were not usable or used. I did sexualize Trantor somewhat, more than what the script necessarily indicated.

One of my favorite lines that I've ever gotten to say in a film is "Come on, baby, jump it."

WN: What did you learn from being in *Galaxy of Terror?*

GZ: Not my first, but one of my first #MeToo experiences had to do with Ray Walston. One day he just came up to me and said, "My car's in the shop. Would you mind driving me home?" I said, "Of course I will; I would be glad to." I drove him home and then came the request through my agent: would I pick him up for the next day's shooting and then drive him home? This went on for many days. One day we got to his house, and he said, "My wife is off doing something or other; would you like to come in and have some lunch?" I had been getting and ignoring a few other little signals before then. I just was not comfortable saying that I would love to do that. I said, "No, I can't. I've got to get home." He treated me badly after that.

When I think of what I learned, it was sort of a reinforcement of don't mess around that way. Don't get yourself into these situations. He had someone at home. I had someone at home. It's not my thing to get involved with people in some casual way. I understand what happens. I understand that there are women who are at a stage in their lives or in their careers when they feel that they need something that, say, the star can give them. I never have felt that way—ever. I've never been tempted. It was repugnant to me, whether or not it would have helped me professionally. that's one thing that I learned: how to say "No."

WN: Did you ever have an opportunity to teach or suggest anything to anyone involved with making *Galaxy of Terror?*

GZ: Knowing me I'm sure I did, but I have blessedly forgotten.

WN: As the crew lifts off for Morganthus, Captain Trantor only gives them thirty seconds to get buckled up for takeoff, explaining that "Seconds wasted here could be costing lives on Morganthus." She also states, "If we have to get there at all, we might as well get there fast." Is the concern for the lives on Morganthus the real or only reason for being in a rush? In the extras, you speak of Trantor's need "to assert her own authority."

GZ: This is what I think I thought: "Her fast pace is masking her fear of this mission. She has trauma that she has not processed from being the lone survivor of the Hesperus massacre. She has these terrible fears, so her attitude is kind of "This will probably not go well, so let's get it over with." There's a sort of an assumed macho-ness to mask her own feeling of extreme vulnerability. That includes leaving in an unsafe manner. That's what I decided was going on with her.

One of the things an actor has to do is take the things that she doesn't understand and make sense of them. The actor's job is to understand why you are saying every syllable that you utter, what you are really thinking when you say that—the subtext. And you must make up shit to fill those gaps because nobody's going to tell you what your subtext is. Not only that, it's not even their business to tell you. The writer can't tell you that. The director can't tell you that. The very first time you say a speech or even a word that you don't really understand why you are saying it.... I will know when I watch that. When people have asked me to work with them on a scene, that's what I tell them. I will stop them and say, "What does that word mean?" They'll say, "I don't know." I'll say, "I'm asking you because I can tell you don't know." They'll say, "How? How can you tell?" And I'll answer, "Well, because your energy leaves you, in a certain way." There's a change in your energy when you don't know what the fuck you're talking about. Even if you don't know that you don't know that, I can see it, and the audience will see it. They won't know why, but their interest drops when your energy changes. All kinds of interesting things happen when you're watching actors.

WN: What's it like being a woman making movies in the 1980s?

GZ: I've touched on this some, but here's another example. Larry Schiller directed *The Executioner's Song* (1982). I went in for the role of Kathryne Baker, a housedress kind of lady, poor and sort of downtrodden. I went in and did the audition in a housedress I kept in the closet for such occasions. My agent called and said, "They like what you did more than any other reader by far, but he wants you to come in looking a bit more sexy." I said, "But that's not the character." My agent is already bored, and he says, "Just do it." I get this black and white zebra pattern dress with a tight belt and stiletto heels. I walk in, and there's Larry Schiller and a bunch of guys sitting around him. I saunter into the room with one hand on my hip. I am definitely playing the outfit. He goes, "Well, what is this?" And I say, with a big smile on my face, "*This* is my fuck-you-Larry-Schiller dress." There was this beat of silence, which I was ready for. Then he burst out laughing and all of the guys burst out laughing. I got the role. That's me being an actress in the 1980s.

WN: What do you think about the maggot sex scene?

GZ: I think the maggot sex scene was just fine. Good God, this is genre. Frankly, I find the director's distaste kind of pretentious. I don't know what to make of his reaction. Really? He wanted to do a "tasteful version?" I don't get it.

WN: It is a horror film.

GZ: There you go. I thought it was great, and I think Taaffe O'Connell did a bang-up job as Dameia, as did everyone who was involved in making that scene work. I think it helped sell the movie.

WN: It was shocking then. Do you think it's still shocking now?

GZ: If you were to take it just by itself along with scenes from other films since then, maybe not so much. In the context of that whole film, though, it is still somewhat shocking.

WN: There's a lot of horrific, grisly things in the film but, that scene is probably the peak moment of horror in the film. The scene still stands out, though maybe not as much as it once did.

GZ: I find another scene potentially more shocking. That is the scene where Ranger becomes two people, two selves confronting and fighting with one another. That really deserved better. We should have seen better close-ups of both of those selves. If more time had been given to that scene, it would have been quite frightening—it would have made us examine ourselves.

WN: In the extras, the director, Bruce D. Clark, says that "the part she had was not well-written," and the character had "some pretty dreadful lines." What do you think?

GZ: Besides the "Come on, baby, jump it" line, I had other lines that I rather liked. I disagree that I had terrible lines. Now, we all had some very difficult lines—that's for sure. I rather liked the odd things that people say in this movie, and, by and large, I thought the actors handled those lines fine. I don't think I had more odd speeches than the others. It makes me nervous when he says "She had a lot of bad lines to say." I just can't help but feel that if I'd managed them better, he wouldn't have thought that.

WN: So you put the responsibility more on yourself than the script.

GZ: I do. I can't really see that I managed them badly, though. What I think happened here is that at some point he thought to himself, "Man, there're some terrible lines here," and he couldn't imagine how anybody was going to say them. He never had the moment of saying, "Yeah, but she is handling it." There was the writer, Marc Siegler, and there was the director,

Bruce D. Clark. Roger Corman says in the extras that they wrote together. They may have had issues in certain areas. What Bruce said could have been an artifact from stuff that had gone on between them during the writing. My memory is that Siegler was around, by the way, and I didn't know then that that wasn't the usual way to run a shoot. They usually try to keep the writer offset during filming.

WN: Why is that?

GZ: It's just sort of the way it's done in Hollywood. The actors could go up to the writer and say, "What exactly did you mean here? Is the way I'm doing it what you imagined?" They want the director to get those questions. Anyway, if I were watching the movie, I would not single out Captain Trantor as having worse lines to deliver than any of the other characters.

WN: There are certainly some memorable lines. Can you tell us what these three lines mean? "An oxer in a breather bar," "Fame is the food that dead men eat" and "The master sends meat, but the devil sends cooks."

GZ: I don't remember asking what those lines meant. I remember knowing that I had to decide what they meant. So: "An oxer in a breather bar"—that was easy. I decided it was related to the fact that there are now bars where you go in and take oxygen. "Oxer" refers to someone who is into oxygen. "Fame is the food that dead men eat" is a way of saying that lasting fame really comes only after death. "The master sends meat, but the devil sends cooks" means we can thank God for our food, but the devil sure can fuck it up. As we learn, the Planet Master *is* God, in a sense. The quote presupposes a culture in which the Planet Master is indeed God in terms of what their concept of God is. That's a huge thing to understand.

WN: *Galaxy of Terror* was the only film you made with Corman? Why?

GZ: He didn't ask me to do another that I recall, but if he did call me to do something else and I couldn't for some reason, then I would have forgotten it.

WN: How did you think *Galaxy of Terror* would end up doing in the box office?

GZ: I can only say that it probably wound up in the end doing better that I'd imagined it would.

WN: Did you have low expectations?

GZ: To say that I had low expectations might seem to imply that I did it with less than my full heart and soul, which I did not because I don't know how to. I don't know how to work less hard when I'm being paid less money. I've never been able to do that or wanted to do that. I had no idea that it would find its place as a cult film.

WN: What did you think *Galaxy of Terror* would do for your own career?

GZ: I hoped it would somehow show the film world that I could do that kind of character.

WN: What did you think critics would think of *Galaxy of Terror?*

GZ: I can't imagine that I thought it would get much of a critical response of any kind.

WN: You didn't think it was Oscar-worthy?

GZ: No. But neither do I think "Oscar-worthy" necessarily suggests nothing but good things about a movie.

WN: The booklet included with the *Galaxy of Terror* DVD states that it has been listed in the top fifty worst movies of all time. Is this fair?

GZ: It's uninformed. I'm not really into fair or unfair, frankly.

WN: You said that "This has cult classic written all over it." What are the trademarks of a cult classic, and how does *Galaxy of Terror* fulfill them?

GZ: This is one of those films that justifies the category of So Bad It's Good. There is a category of films that encompasses a lot of so-called "cult films," where you find yourself laughing at a lot of stuff that you suspect wasn't meant to be funny.

WN: Can it also be that it has a longer life than people may have anticipated? Decades later are people still watching it, talking about it, studying it, analyzing it, asking questions about it?

GZ: The proof is in the pudding when it comes to a cult film.

WN: Do you think a cult film is one that exerts influence later on? Do you think any other films were influenced by *Galaxy of Terror?*

GZ: I don't know. It seems to me that there were a few that have been influenced in certain ways by it. It's hard to say. I think a lot of the techniques they developed in response to shortages of time, materials, money and other resources got out before the crew went on record explaining how they did certain things.

WN: I think of *The Rocky Horror Picture Show* (1975) as possibly the ultimate cult film. Objectively it's kind of bad, but there is something that still resonates or shines through. Even though it's maybe not the best film, there's something stylistically significant or important about it, and we still respond to it. If it's really a bad movie that offers nothing, you don't respond to it. It's like when people have ugly Christmas sweater parties. It's remarkable for some reason.

GZ: I like that.

WN: Maybe it has something to do with failure or incompleteness. There's something about these things that we connect with. Maybe it's because we can identify more with something flawed than we can with something that's perfectly done and well-executed.

GZ: Yeah. Like not just a moment, but a whole script that slips on a banana peel.

WN: It's a breach of expectations, maybe. That taps into humor and also horror.

GZ: Okay! This is good stuff.

WN: Does the film have a message?

GZ: It has more than its share, doesn't it? There was a time in filmmaking when it was no longer cool for a film to have a "message." I don't know when that became an unwritten rule. We used to laughingly say "If anybody asks you what the film is about, just tell them it's about corridors and tentacles." But there is more to it than that. I cannot tell you what each and every character was afraid of and, therefore, what killed him or her. I don't think it's clear in every case. At any rate, it does seem to echo something like "The only thing we have to fear is fear itself." That seems to be one very clear, firm message. What else do you think?

WN: Fear is definitely a core element or theme. Roger Corman and others have talked extensively about that, as well. Maybe there is something there about groups, unity and working together, because it seems that as people split off they begin to be picked off. That's kind of a classic device in horror films. I'm also thinking about how Cabren becomes the new master, and there is something there about Cabren ultimately becoming what he fears. I'm also thinking about how we seek to overthrow or conquer something, but we have to be careful that when we overthrow it or conquer it that we don't put something just as bad or worse in its place. Sometimes that thing that can be just as bad or worse is us, the ones who think we are heroes.

GZ: Okay, but I don't think the film says that. I agree with what you're saying, but I don't think the film says it. I think the film goes no further than to say that because Cabren has at every step mastered his fear he has now unwittingly made himself Planet Master because as soon as he had passed every test the energy went out of the Planet Master and he was now only an old man. I don't believe that we are to think as we watch the film that this change is a bad thing for him. I think we see him accept it and don't see a point when we are to think "Oh, my God, what have we wrought here?"

WN: So the end isn't horrific. It's kind of noble in that reading because Cabren passes the test, purifies himself of his fear and attains a higher consciousness—sort of like a Grail quest with Percival and Lancelot.

GZ: Yes, like that. All that. I think that's as far as the film goes. I may be wrong. I don't think he tells us that he is now an evil person.

WN: No. We just make that assumption that the Planet Master is this evil entity that needs to be defeated. Maybe not, then.

GZ: I think we are to be very wary of the Planet Master, but at the end we are supposed to see that he's been doing his job, but he's an old man and needs to pass the torch. Most likely he had an idea of who would be his successor, but he had to make sure and put everyone through this ordeal to be certain.

WN: The point of this is it's a long test and series of trials that the Planet Master conducts in order to find or at least verify a replacement.

GZ: Yes. I would say that what *Galaxy of Terror* does is sort of embody in its thrust, text and acting the idea that who we want as a leader is someone who does not want to be the leader.

WN: Because if someone wants to be leader, that person wants it for power, personal gain or some other ulterior motive. People who don't want to be leaders realize the amount of personal sacrifice that being a good leader actually entails...

GZ: Yes, but not only the personal sacrifice. They also don't in any way really want to tell other people what to do, but they are leaders and they can't help that. If you notice, Cabren took over the role of leader even though Baelon was saying, "I'm in charge here." Cabren would always bend to that until finally, to get people through the latter portions of this journey, he did have to assume the role of leader and so he did.

WN: It's an organic transition into that leadership position. He's not elected or chosen or appointed; it's just the natural order of things.

GZ: So in a way it says, "Beware of those who wish to lead or some version of that. Look for those who do not want the mantle."

WN: I've thought about the movie a lot in connection with the theme of fear—because that's what everyone talks about—but not leadership so much.

Next time I watch I am going to go into *Galaxy of Terror* with a new sense of it and look for different things.

GZ: When I was watching the very end of the film last night, I realized that I had seen the end but had forgotten it somehow. I would give anything to see the film reedited someday.

WN: What are the changes you would want to see in a reedited version?

GZ: That scene with Ranger that we talked about could have been done so much better. Robert Englund's work was aces, but whether writing or coverage or editing or some combination was at fault, I can't say. That should have been a really great scene, but we've been told that they don't have anything; they got rid of everything that wasn't actually in the film. Whether it's four frames or one frame, it's all gone now. So there's no reediting to be done, I would say.

WN: Any other examples from your career?

GZ: I've had that happen a few times, most memorably with *Wild at Heart* (1990), which we shot right after the first season of *Twin Peaks*, and I played crazy Juana. We had this team of three assassins, and we killed Harry Dean Stanton, who played Johnnie Farragut. I had this really long scene where I pace up and down. He's bound up, white tape over his mouth, and we are going to kill him, but God forbid we just kill him. I kiss him on that tape, which leaves a pair of red lips on it for the whole scene. I think it's nine pages of me and my club foot and my cane, and I'm pacing up and down saying, "First I'm going to touch this, and then I'm going to go over there and touch that, and then...." Just on and on with this. Psychological torture. When they went to look for that footage for the reissue, it was long gone. That's what happens after years, and sometimes it's too bad. Well, it was cut because the preview audiences included a few who complained of heart palpitations and one guy who said he was having a heart attack. But some of that might have been fun for extras in the reissue.

I was shocked at realizing how many of the cast of *Galaxy of Terror* died really young. I looked up every person in the cast on IMDb and found who was still alive and who was not. A couple of them just died last year. The causes of their deaths were listed for two of them. One was lung cancer. That's possibly smoking. Another was small cell squamous throat cancer. And that's possibly smoking. Here I am still smoking.

WN: How long have you smoked?

GZ: Forever. We'll see how I do. Anything else?

WN: In the extras, you said that "the movie will be remembered many years for a number of things." What are the things you remember about *Galaxy of Terror?* After watching it again, what stands out to you?

GZ: I understand why it has become a bit of a cult classic. I'm not surprised. I can see why it is regarded that way as opposed to "Why the hell is anyone still talking about this?" I'm really glad I got to do it. I'm really glad that my friend Carol Caldwell inappropriately tarted me up for that audition. I'm glad that I listened to her and let her do that against what seemed like my better judgment at the time. I'm glad I got to play that character and work with all those people.

ALLAN HOLZMAN

Interview by Stephen B. Armstrong

STEPHEN B. ARMSTRONG: I should tell you that I saw *Mutant*, your director's cut of what Roger Corman ultimately released as *Forbidden World* (1982), the other night. And the last ten minutes or so I felt absolutely stressed. It was so intense—the flickering editing.

ALLAN HOLZMAN: There's a funny story about the subliminal sequence in the end, the mutant's death once the vomiting occurs. He just has to die off, but it wasn't originally fulfilling enough of an ending, in my opinion. I was searching for a way to have it visually more exciting. In film, when you make lots of small cuts and you're trimming, you have to be sure that the codes are connected to the small trims. There are two kinds of codes. There's one that the lab has, and there's one that you apply. They're each a foot apart. There's always some area that doesn't have some codes, so when you work fast you don't scribe it in. You have a lot of unmarked small trims, and you collect those over time just to have them. So I asked the assistant to splice together all the small trims, and these are one- and two- and three-frame trims. A lot of one-frame trims. I said, "Don't worry about the order. Just splice them all together." It took her three days, and it was this collection of great subliminal movements that I shaped to get inside the mutant's mind.

SA: When the Jesse Vint character wakes up at the start of the film a similar sort of sequence occurs.

AH: We had no money to start to do the opening of a movie. The only material I had once the film was shot was the movie itself, and so I thought, "Well, I will have him flash forward in a dream." It went exactly with *Beethoven's Piano Concerto No. 1.* it was great to have a flurry of movement there. There's an interesting story, though, that I don't think you're aware of. After directing *Mutant*, and editing it, Roger hired me to do the trailer for *Fitzcarraldo* (1982). The central theme in that was the opera; so when I cut the trailer, one of the long notes was given a long stream of subliminal edits that were very expressive. But Roger hired his new head of marketing, Elliot Slutzky, from Chicago. He said, "It will never play in the mini-malls." I said, "Well, it's *Fitzcarraldo*. It's not a mass market film." I won the argument until I went to the mix and Roger called me. It was at a payphone on La Brea. He said, "I'm agreeing with Elliot." I told Roger that I could no longer work for him after that.

SA: Wow. Roger's editing over your editing—or his rejections of some of your decisions in the cutting room—that prompted a split?

AH: Definitely. It wasn't so much about the editing itself; it was the content. He loved my editing. It was the idea of having all this art film editing going on when you're trying to appeal to eighteen- and nineteen-year-olds. That was the time when they didn't think that kind of movie would appeal to the youth market. Obviously subliminal editing is used a lot now. I had started with subliminal editing in college when I taught myself film. I was the school projectionist, so I had the equipment to splice and project; during the winter work term, I cut together white leader and black leader to music, actually to the Beatles' "White Album." That's how I learned film editing.

SA: You did rock music videos later, I recall: Berlin's "Masquerade," Tim Scott's "High Hopes" and Susan Justin's "Woman in the Window." Music has really been a part of your work for much of your career.

AH: Always. I was a Bob Dylan fanatic from the get-go. I even marched with him in the first anti-Vietnam War March on Washington, D.C., in 1965. I actually directed a play at Café Figaro where he often performed. I was in Cleveland at college when he had his first rock band concert tour. It was just awful!

SA: The name of the college in Cleveland was—?

AH: Western Reserve University before it merged with Case Institute of Technology.

SA: How did you migrate to Los Angeles?

AH: When I reached my junior year as a math major, we were told that what we were studying, the fourth dimension, did not apply to life. Since I stuttered, teaching was not exactly on my radar for career choices. A group of Antioch students came to Cleveland to produce their anti-war plays and cast me as the lead. I had often pursued acting as a creative outlet since stutterers don't stutter when they act. So I left college to study acting at Circle in the Square in New York City. They gave me a scholarship to Williamstown Summer Theater in the Berkshires in northern Massachusetts, where I was offered a full scholarship and work stipend for a three-year program at Bennington College, where I graduated in 1970. At Bennington I fell in love with theater directing, and since my job was the school's projectionist, I received an amazing film education showing a feature every weekend from the Janus archive. Since I had film equipment, I taught myself editing. My goal was to earn money as a film editor and produce my own plays. And then I started really falling in love with film. When I returned to New York after Bennington, there was a Samurai film festival with a new double bill every three days that was truly inspiring. I worked as both an assistant editor and editor. My first feature, *Confusion's Circle* (1974) for John Avnet, starred Richard Gere. It never came out. But I suggested to John that he go to film school, and after he got into AFI, he encouraged me to take the plunge. I applied. I went out there in fall of 1973. There were twenty students at that time: ten in directing, and the others were producers, writers and directors of photography.

SA: You were studying directing at that point.

AH: Yes. I had directed quite a bit of theater, and I had made three short films. Two of the films I combined into one called "WAR," depicting a soldier's erotic fantasy at his point of death. It won the Brooklyn Arts and Cultural Foundation Film Festival in 1971 and toured colleges with the best of the first annual New York Erotic Film Festival. There was a screening of "WAR" as part of the Brooklyn Arts and Cultural Association at the Metropolitan Museum of Art. When the erotic imagery came up, all the mothers grabbed their children, covered their eyes and tried to pull them out of the theater. There was this huge congestion at the exit. But the film was so short—it was only two-and-a-half minutes long—and by the time they reached the doorway, it was over, and everyone started coming back. I didn't even get a chance to see my movie!

SA: So you were in avant-garde circles at that point and somehow wound up at New World?

AH: When I went to AFI, I didn't really have enough money to get through my time there, so I needed editing work. A friend of mine, Barbara

Noble, who graduated from NYU, had met Julie Corman at some party or function. Julie had asked her to edit, and since she was a student and didn't really need extra money at that point, she recommended me. She knew that I needed money. Julie was producing her first movie, which was *Candy Stripe Nurses* (1974). She really liked a short film I had edited called "Sand" that was about a sand sculpture made and destroyed in one day when the tide rolled in. It was just music and film. She loved that.

SA: Did you cut *Candy Stripe Nurses* in the editing suites of Jack Rabin and Associates?

AH: Yes. Jack gave Roger free editing room in exchange for all the optical work. Everyone cut there. Trailers, as well.

SA: Who were some of the people you were cutting with or interacting with?

AH: On *Candy Stripe Nurses*, my assistant was Hal Harrison, who eventually became the head of Paramount Post Production. I think he served in that capacity for about twenty years, maybe even longer. I didn't have a lot of interaction with many people on the film crew because I just worked in the editing room. I didn't really hang out with the film crew at al. Since I was also a student, I had to go back and forth between film school and working for Roger. Ironically, I had to keep quiet that I was spending time with either one because I had to earn full participatory credit from each place. They also had absolutely no respect for each other. Film students thought that Roger Corman films were beneath them creatively, and all the Roger Corman people disdained film students for their snobbery and lack of professional filmmaking experience. I kept quiet and just did the work.

SA: You must have been having twenty-hour days.

AH: I found that a Jack in the Box fish sandwich, milkshake and one cup of coffee could keep me up all night. I'm almost convinced there was amphetamine in the milkshake or the frozen fish. Honestly.

SA: You did another project with Julie—*Crazy Mama.*

AH: That was Julie's second film. I had finished shooting my AFI film, which was *Skin*, in 1974, based on a story by Roald Dahl. I ran out of money once again, and I needed another editing job and called Julie to see if she had any work, and she did. Jonathan Demme directed *Crazy Mama*, but originally the director was Shirley Clarke, who had directed *Portrait of Jason*, a really great documentary. Shirley Clarke chose to keep her dental appointment instead of the casting session, so Julie fired her and hired Jonathan just two weeks prior to the start of shooting, which was a big shock to everyone. Jonathan had just directed *Caged Heat* for Roger, so he was their hot director.

SA: Tell me about how the cutting went on a picture like *Crazy Mama*. You cut black-and-white footage, right?

AH: It always worked the same way for Roger's films. All the dailies were black and white. You didn't see color until you attended the Hollywood premiere. Having the work print in black and white saved quite of bit of money. You would do a few color tests for the first day's shoot to make sure the color was coming out correctly and then black and white. Jonathan wanted me fired the day that he got hired. He wanted to bring his own editor.

SA: How did you stand up to that? Did Julie intervene?

AH: She and Roger said they wanted me. Jonathan never liked me. It was not a pleasant experience.

SA: I think that movie is cut very well.

AH: I remember Joe Dante telling me that at the screening because he had heard all the things that were being said about me. He really liked it. I wasn't really friends with him. He just came up to me and said that. From the outset, I felt that the pacing needed to be faster, and Jonathan wanted to slow things down and hold in one shot longer and that sort of thing. I felt that as an action-comedy it really needed to move quicker.

SA: You have that opening sequence, a sort of prologue, and there's this jump in time that's almost disorienting, but it makes you, or makes me, at least, lean forward and say, "Hey what's going on here?"

AH: I fell in love with second unit. The footage was shot by Tak Fujimoto. And it was directed by Jonathan's wife, Evelynn Purcell. I used a lot of it, and it really drove a lot of action in the film. The interesting thing is that Jonathan went on to hire Tak as cinematographer for all of his movies after that, but I received hell for liking second unit at the time.

SA: Demme has this persona of being an easygoing, likeable guy.

AH: He was with everyone but me. I didn't befriend him. But I didn't make it easy for him, either. I wasn't the easiest person to work with. I didn't really budge that much if I strongly believed in something. He was the same way. I'm sure in the future that he had control of the editing because he also produced. I can understand from his point of view why he didn't like me. But, still, it's hard to explain why you're not liked.

SA: Following *Crazy Mama* your work went in new directions. You followed another path, right?

AH: I showed Roger the film I made at AFI with the hope of getting a directing break. He had hired me after *Crazy Mama* to recut or, rather, to take ten or fifteen minutes out of a Peter O'Toole movie, *The Other Side of*

Paradise, that he'd purchased. I screened my recut for him, and that was at a classic screening room Nosseck's on Sunset Boulevard near Beverly Hills. The elderly Nosseck died last year. His son Noel Nosseck is a director. I think they were in operation seventy or eighty years—some remarkable amount—and it was just in the back of a row of small buildings where Dick Clark had his production offices. It only sat about fifteen or twenty people. That's where you saw dailies, as well, during the first week of shooting, and maybe once a week the crew was invited on a Friday night to see dailies. So I showed Roger my AFI graduation film, Skin. He only fell asleep once during that—I reached over, pretending to raise the sound, so that I could wake him up. Afterwards as I was carrying my film can out to the street, we stopped and I said, "Can I di... Can I di... Can I di...?" Finally, he bowed his head slightly and said, "Thank you very much, Allan, I'll see you later." I watched him walk away. I hadn't even been able to say the word "direct." that sent me on a different path. I realized that I'd closed off my era at New World. I went on to become an action editor, always trying to make my own films and develop my scripts.

Then that world fell apart a few years later, and I needed to rethink my life. I decided to give up directing and pursue the path of editing. I wrote Roger a letter asking him to recommend me to Coppola to edit *Hammett* (1982). I was really excited by Wim Wenders's work, and I'm from Baltimore. The action films I cut were for Fred Weintraub, who was the producer of *Enter the Dragon* (1973) and *Woodstock* (1969). I cut three films for him: *It's Showtime* (1976), *Checkered Flag or Crash* (1977) and *The Amsterdam Kill* (1977). Rudy Fehr was the head of post at Warner Brothers. I was on the Warner lot, and I was cutting in the building where Rudy worked, where Marcia Lucas was cutting *Taxi Driver* (1976), and Robert Wolfe was cutting *All the President's Men* (1976). I was the only one there with a KEM, an acronym for Keller-Elektro-Mechanik, a flatbed editing machine, showing them how it worked.

Anyway, Roger said that he hadn't talked to Coppola in a while, like three months. Roger and Francis had been next door neighbors when they were both living in Beverly Glen. They were very close. But Roger continued our conversation with an offer. "I'm doing my biggest movie ever, *Battle Beyond the Stars.* John Sayles wrote the script. I'd really like you to edit it. Can you do it? Can you come into the office right away?" So I came into the office. The rest is history.

SA: Hadn't you worked on *Smokey Bites the Dust* (1981) a bit?

AH: That was after *Battle Beyond the Stars.*

SA: Yikes! That was after?

AH: You've confused your New World history. The interesting thing was that the producer of *Smokey Bites the Dust* was the production manager on *Battle.*

SA: Gale Anne Hurd.

AH: Yes.

SA: Let's get back to *Battle Beyond the Stars.* It's a well-known movie: *Seven Samurai* meets *Star Wars* (1977), with Jim Cameron handling the art.

AH: Let me tell you the Jim Cameron story. It's in my book based on a journal that I had kept during the entire editing process, *Celluloid Wars: Welcome to the Roger Corman School of Filmmaking.* With *2001*, Kubrick had been the first person to use front projection instead of rear screen. We were trying to replicate that on *Battle.* We had a French cinematographer, Daniel Lacambre, and they worked out the tests, and the tests were okay. But when they shot it the next day, the background came out too dark, and this was not something that you could fix in post. Everything was front-screened in front of the camera, where the background image is projected onto the actors as well as on the screen. The light on the actors is strong enough to wipe out the projected image. The screen itself is covered with thousands of tiny prisms that redirect the beam of light directly into the camera lens so you are getting maximum reflection off the screen. But the image came out dark, way dark, and you couldn't see the background at all.

So I called Roger and said, "The front screen didn't work. It's too dark. They have to reshoot." He said, "I never reshoot. Make it work." Then I walked across the mainstage that night, and it was empty except for this one person bent over this A-frame table, looking down. I walked up to him and asked, "Are you okay?" It was the guy who did the front screen paintings, and this was his last day because, as he told me, his work was over. I looked at the two panoramic landscapes he had painted, and they were just brilliant, just amazing futuristic visions. When I asked the producer Mary Ann Fisher for Roger's number, she declined. "Roger does not like being disturbed during dinner." I was totally insistent upon reaching him to tell him how great the paintings were, and that they had to reshoot whatever it cost. When I reached him, he responded firmly with a calmness that was absolute. "Allan, I'm having dinner right now. I want you to listen. For the last time: I never reshoot. Make it work." I said, "We've got to at least hire this guy—it's his last day— he could design a set or something." Roger responded, "Okay, what's his name?" I asked the guy. "Jim Cameron," he answered. Roger hired him to design the set for the Nanelia character when Cayman has her imprisoned, hanging by her hands, with steam rising beneath her. That's where he used the lunch boxes and egg crates for the futuristically textured walls of the set.

SA: You were going through Dumpsters and pulling out Styrofoam boxes for that?

AH. No, no, no. We got new boxes from a factory in Long Beach.

SA: That's just crazy that someone from the cutting room is actually there doing production design at the same time, and all of these things are fluid.

AH: I was desperate, professionally, to have a film that really worked.

I was so tired of making films better. Once mediocre, always mediocre. A mediocre film could be a much-improved mediocre film that moves well, but it never gets really good. That was a term I embraced—that "I was really great at turning shit into mediocrity." I was tired of that. So, with *Battle*, I tried from the outset to have something good, and I took the responsibility to make sure whatever I could do, I did. Whatever it took, I would find a way to do it

SA: Tell me about the process of editing. There were two of you. You took the first third and the latter third of the footage?

AH: I was hired to be the editor. In those days with film editing you couldn't possibly keep up with camera, which Roger wanted. With *Crazy Mama*, for instance, there was a second editor, Lewis Teague, who went on to direct *Lady in Red*. You had a second editor and usually that editor gets assigned the middle three reels. The main editor takes the responsibility for the first and third acts. Then as soon as the first cut is finished, the first editor takes over the whole thing and makes the changes for the entire film. The second editor is really there to get the film up as soon as possible after shooting. Usually within a few days. Then Roger wastes no time firing the second editor and keeping the first. He takes out the additional Moviola. If you were staying and working all night alone, which I did a lot, you would then no longer have the use of the second editor's Moviola. There was a point on *Battle* when he took out the water from our room to save money. I made a chart of observed activity of the people in the editing room going to the main stage to get water, and showed him how long that actually took and proved that he was losing money that way. So he put the water back.

SA: Tell me how you moved from *Battle Beyond the Stars* on to *Mutant* with *Smokey Bites the Dust* in-between.

AH: On *Battle* there was real friction between me and the head of special effects, Chuck Kaminski, who is still working with Cameron and has worked on most of his movies, I believe. Day one on *Battle*, he came over to me and said that I wasn't, as the editor, going to get any of his footage because he had been screwed over by too many editors in the past. I said, "Well, that may be the case, but there is no way I can edit a movie without incorporating your footage into the live action. At some point, I'm going to have to get it. If you give it to me now, I'll have more time to work with it."

During the production and post-production, I kept saying that they weren't able to do all of the spaceship action as written in the script. John Sayles crafted brilliant action, but any choreography that involved more than one ship in the shot had not been composited. They were churning out great fly-bys. I'll admit they were working out the technology on a really inexpensive level. But when the Elicon motion control first came out, there were lots of flaws. In addition, it was quite a challenge to get the movement in the starfield right as the ships fly by. Roger needed to see numbers every day. Every morning his assistant called to ask how many shots the effects people shot. Roger received a report of six or seven shots with no description. I kept saying, "They aren't doing it. It's not really coming in."

At one point I was instructed that I was getting in the way and interfering. They wanted me creatively, but I "should take a backseat since all of live action had been edited, and let the second editor Bob Kizer take over. You know, he's the technical expert," they reminded me. I was anti-slugs. I refused to cut them in. I wouldn't compromise because I said that slugs make you think that something will be there, and I didn't think it was going to be accomplished by the film's release date. I edited the film in ways the scene works without inserts, without the slugs. It still needed the excitement of effects shots, but the continuity of the scene had been established. That argument was a wash. They insisted on slugs, and Bob cut them in.

SA: So what you had was something that was heavy on talking and human talent, and they wanted leader in between.

AH: Yes. Bob would put all the leader in with all the numbers, and we would have a screening. He read like a hundred things off his clipboard in two hours. People were really impressed that they were seeing all that action without seeing anything on the screen. That had to go another three weeks before anyone realized the effects shots were not coming up, that they were seeing the same leader. By that time, Roger had let Bob go. I saw Roger walking really depressed in the parking lot. I asked him what was the matter. He told me that he had to do another delay, and he wasn't going to make the summer release. We were trying to come out at the same time as *The Empire Strikes Back*. I think *Empire* was at the beginning of the summer of 1980, and we were at the end of the summer, and if we were going to be much later, we may not be the first rip-off of *Star Wars*.

So I said that if he gave me total control I could make it work. I would restructure the choreography of the battles and make them all suicide runs to the main ship, which the special effects crew—hired by Chuck and led by designers and model makers Bob and Denis Skotak—had practically done anyway. There were so many beautifully shot flybys that I could intercut with character shots that I could pull from other scenes. I said, "The key is to have a choreographed display of laser beams. But I have to have control over every department. I can't have anyone objecting to anything that I say that I want to do." And he said, "Okay, I've got your back on that. Use my name for whatever you need to do. Go for it." And I did. Right away I got resistance from the rotoscope department, saying, "You have to have realistic laser beams. You can't have them coming out of camera and blocking out the frame."

I had learned about whiting out the frame when I was editing for Roger at Jack Rabin's optical house. Joe Dante and Allan Arkush, who were editing trailers at the time, had what they called the Dante-Arkush Memorial Library—reels of film from labs that they were going to throw out but instead sold cheaply for editors to fill the space between effects without having to buy expensive leader. Sometimes a classic reel would come in and Allan and Joe would save it on a shelf under their editing table. One reel was the bridge sequence from Sam Peckinpah's *Wild Bunch* (1969), which I carefully studied. At the peak of the explosion, there would just be as much as three frames or four frames of pure clear. Then you would see some yellow emerge in the frame. And I went, "Boy, I can add those clear frames to our explosions, which are not as big. But with additional clear frames and a big sound effect, the production value shoots way up." I started adding clear frames to every gunshot or explosion and making it bigger and adding more sound, and that's what I did with all the laser beams in *Battle*. I stayed up for four weeks, and I'm talking four weeks of not sleeping. Obviously, I slept in the editing room for a couple hours at a time, and I would get a few hours after a shower at home, but I was on burnout.

I was ruthless. But I got it done. And *Battle* opened on time and was successful financially and critically. Roger owed me. He asked me eight times to cut *Galaxy of Terror*. I said, "Roger, I've done it all for you as editor. I want my chance to direct."

He finally said, "Can you stutter and direct?"

This is the first time that I've mentioned stuttering in this interview, I think. That's one reason why I got into editing to begin with—it's that I didn't have to talk to anybody. I could express visibly and emotionally; expressing emotions through what you're seeing is how a stutterer lives a lot of his or her life. I answered his question "Can you stutter and direct?" by saying "I do stutter, but it's in the act of communicating. It's less when I'm directing because I'm in control, but I still stutter. But it's in the act of communicating, which is more than most directors do." He said, after thinking a moment, "You have a point there, Allan. I'm going to put you through the Roger Corman School of Filmmaking." And he used Joe and Allan as examples to say that I would start with directing second unit for an upcoming film.

So I called him every week, and finally after two months there was an opening to direct second unit on the car movie *Smokey Bites the Dust*, which Chuck Griffith was directing, and they needed me to shoot the car action as well as edit those scenes. So I did that. And then Roger hired me to do extra scenes for a kung fu movie called *Firecracker* (1981) that Cirio Santiago had directed in the Philippines with an American actress, Jillian Kesner. I did a chase scene and a love scene. I remembered from *Candy Stripe Nurses* the big scene at the end of that movie. Roger always did his movies with three parallel stories so that as soon as one became boring you could cut to the other one. In this one, the candy striper was trying to get this rock star to get it up because he had erectile dysfunction before there was a name like that for it. She succeeds, and he starts making love to her and two go-go dancers. But it's shot in one wide-angle handheld shot, and the guy never takes his pants off, and he dry humps the women. First of all, Roger hates when there's no coverage. He has no opportunity to edit. In those days you could not do a jump cut, so the shot had to stay in as it was. Roger called the director, whose name was Alan Holleb, back into the room for a last meeting. And he said, "Alan, I don't know where you go to from here or what you plan to do, but I want you to remember one thing: when a man fucks, he takes his pants off."

When it came time for me do the love scene in *Firecracker*, I thought, "Oh, I'll have the woman take off the guy's pants with kung fu knives." I read Roger the scene, and he said, "Allan, that's brilliant." For the action scene, I used Roger's lumberyard, which was New World's studio. When Jillian gets out of the cab, it is supposed to take place in the Philippines; but I thought that lumberyards look the same anywhere in the world. So she gets attacked by two guys in New World's lumberyard, and every time they have a skirmish, she loses one article of clothing. I beat Roger's record of eighty-four setups in one day. I reached ninety-three. But he said not to get excited. He told me, "There's someone with one-hundred-and-thirty-five. He had two sets and would call action on one and then run over to the other one to yell 'Cut!'"

Then Roger took me for a walk around the studio as I was finishing up the editing on *Firecracker*—I recut the movie as well and edited the trailer. He said, "You want to direct a whole movie, don't you, Allan?" I said, "Yes." Then he laid out a path that is pure Roger Corman. "There's a spaceship set available for one day." It was Jim Cameron's set of *Galaxy of Terror*. During the week they shot first unit. Saturday they shot second unit. Monday they were redressing it. So the set was standing unused on Sunday. He continued,

"This is Tuesday. If you can write and direct the opening of a space movie that can go anywhere, I'll give you a whole movie. I owe Jesse Vint a movie, and so he would be your astronaut. And Don Olivera came into the office with his robot suit. He offered it to me for free to use in a movie. So I'll give you the actor and the robot."

SA: Don Olivera?

AH: Yes. Don Olivera risked his life for the vomit scene. There's an amazing story behind that.

SA: Tell me.

AH: Oh, I'll get to that in a moment. Roger said that if I needed any inspiration, he'd always wanted to do a version of *Lawrence of Arabia* (1962) in space. I said, "David Lean is my favorite director." And he said, "Then you should have no problem at all." That's why the planet in the film is called Xarbia. For the film's end, Roger came up with the idea to kill the mutant with cancer. We had to put the cancer in the mutant. I had edited in the Philippines and had observed several psychic surgeries and saw how they would pull the tumor out, breaking the muscles with their hands. So I replicated that in the surgery scene and then set the mutant into the battle, and after the astronaut shoves the tumor down his mouth, the mutant throws up and dies. So how do you make throwing up interesting? It had to be exciting and real. We couldn't do any opticals, and CGI effects did not exist then. We had to do everything in camera. Don had developed this formula— it was his idea to have polyurethane foam. The only thing is, if it touches skin it burns right through, so if any of it backfires while he is in the mutant outfit spewing out this pink stuff, he will be burned. The exciting thing was: the polyurethane liquid solidifies immediately when exposed to air. It replicates pink vomit without looking totally gross. The crew and I hid behind Hefty garbage bags and cut holes in the black plastic. We were looking through these holes in garbage bags, protecting ourselves from being hit by this polyurethane spray, but we weren't worried about our eyes.

SA: How was it to have the opportunity to both edit and direct the same film?

AH: Well, whenever I made my own movies, I did that. When I was making shorts, I was always doing that. After *Forbidden World*, it was difficult to get a producer to hire me as the editor, but I would work around that by editing at night for free. Even when I am not hired to do it, I still wind up doing it. My worst time was on *Out of Control* (1985), which was a movie I made for the new New World that bought Roger's company. I wasn't allowed in the editing room, and I had to re-edit that once it was finished.

SA: There's a nutty story about a preview screening of *Mutant*, with punches and sodas being thrown in response to your attempts to weave some comedy into the story.

AH: *An American Werewolf in London* (1981) had just come out and was really inspiring. It was the first movie that really intended to be funny as well as scary. It didn't hold back from ideas that would excite, entertain and be compelling. I had witnessed what Roger did with *Death Race 2000* in 1975, because as I was coming in to edit *Crazy Mama*, I was going into editor Tina Hirsch's cutting room at Jack Rabin's post production house. She was still taking more comedy out of *Death Race*, mourning every loss. Everyone loved Paul Bartel and everything he did. Everyone was feeling pain. But I had to go into her room, and that was painful for her, as well. Anyway, when it came time to do *Mutant*, I knew that you can't possibly have a movie where someone either gets killed every seven or eight minutes or someone is making love every seven or eight minutes—all in one night!—without having a sense of humor as you go along. No matter how well choreographed at storytelling

177

you can be, somebody's going to be dying or almost dying every seven to eight minutes.

You have two elements that you can always play with: suspense and humor, and if you can meld the two a little bit.... It was Frank Capra who said that "If you make them laugh, you have the audience on your side." You have to question that fine line: are they laughing at the movie or with the movie? I didn't care about that. By the early eighties, audiences were beginning to get sophisticated about film, and you could play with it; they could become aware that they were watching a movie. The story is going to be feeding lots of your sensibilities.

James Horner and I got along so well on *Battle*. I was his music editor. He was great to work with. His brother, Christopher Horner, was the production designer of *Mutant*. But I wanted my girlfriend, Susan Justin, who became my wife a year later, to be the composer, not Jamie. It was heartbreaking, but I wanted a pop-new wave score, something that had rock and beat, melody and a sense of humor. I wanted something driving. I believe that the score defines for the audience how they are supposed to feel. if the music is having fun, you're allowed to have fun.

SA: On the DVD release of the film, there're two cuts of *Mutant*, the one that was released theatrically, which has a seventy-seven-minute running time, and a director's cut that runs eighty-five minutes. What's the story behind the different cuts?

AH: Roger would screen the cuts in his office at New World in a tiny room adjacent to the storage space. It only sat eight people max. He would alternate his staff for each screening and only screen the film four times. I asked everyone in the screening never to laugh except for his story people, whom I could not ask, and only one of those would come at a time; and they were always very serious. No one ever heard any laughter during the screenings, though there was one point when one of the projectionists was commenting on the film. She was going, "Is this the film they shot in twenty days? It is so much fun! Why are they screaming so much?" I didn't anticipate that Roger would "sneak preview" the movie. I hadn't experienced that in any of my editing with him.

He snuck it into what is now a multiplex but which was then the seven-hundred seat Culver Theatre. The audience had come to see, I believe, a movie called *Moving Violations*. The sneak was a surprise. Roger only had a small cardboard rectangular sign written with a felt pen: *"MUTANT:* SNEAK PREVIEW TONIGHT." I swear it was no more than ten inches high and maybe a foot-and-a-half wide. That was it. people were surprised they were seeing a double feature, with the film they were not coming to see screened first. I was standing on the back. I was just on cloud nine. People were screaming and laughing and having a great time yelling back at the screen. The audience was animated. Alive. It was so great.

About two-thirds of the way through, Roger suddenly and with determination comes storming up the aisle, walks right past me. There's a guy in the back of the theater, yelling and screaming. Roger stands over him, and at the precise moment that he is about to yell at the screen, Roger punches him hard right in the face. Roger had his head of post, Clark Henderson, with him. Roger folds his arms and instructs his victim, "Stop laughing! This is a serious sci-fi movie." The audience continues going nuts, so Roger moves away from his unsuspecting target and finds another seat with Clark. I found out years later that they were actually afraid the guy who Roger punched was going to come after him. Anyway, at the end of the screening, Roger stormed out of the theater, saying, "Allan, this is the worst sneak I've had in twenty-three years. But don't worry, I know how to save it." I said, "Save it? It was great." And we argued outside the theater good comedy versus bad comedy. And all the people under thirty were going, "It's okay. It's good." And all the people over thirty, all the sales people, were going, "It will never play in Poughkeepsie. It will never play at the drive-in."

Roger's philosophy is simple and consistently clear. "Don't mix genres. Don't give people anything other than what they expect because then they won't come the next night." If you do something like I was doing, it has to be done well or it will fall flat completely, and he could not depend on the audiences reacting that way. He had learned from his own films at the end of his directing career that when he varied from the genre, as he'd done with *The Trip*—that even though he'd attempted to make a good movie, and it was a good movie, it didn't make money. At any rate, all the young people were saying it was great, and the older people were saying it won't play in the small towns and rural cities. Roger never wanted to depend on good reviews or good word of mouth. He made his money on being in town for a week, and if a picture did well, then he held it for another week. As soon as it dropped off, he left town. He would make two-hundred prints, and those were circulated across the country.

So when Roger finished with the good-comedy-versus-bad-comedy debate, he gave me his final command. "Be in the editing room tomorrow morning to make the cuts, or I'll have someone else do it." As he turned to march away from the movie theater, the guy Roger punched came out with a large Coke and threw it at Roger, hitting him in the back. Roger turned with his fist raised and clenched. When he takes one look at the guy, who's actually bigger than he is, he immediately opens his fists and holds his fingers up and declares, "No, no. We're even."

SA: That's really the strangest story I've heard about Roger Corman.

AH: he sent me to the editing room to make the cuts, and I executed each one seamlessly, arguing and pleading with every loss. We screened it again at a Hollywood Boulevard theater. People still laughed. He told me to make more cuts. I argued every single one, but I was a really good executioner. At the next and final sneak in Torrance, no one came, and Roger declared the movie "locked." But he added insult to injury when he changed the title from *Mutant* to *Forbidden World*. He had asked one of his young female assistants to wait outside Hollywood High and maybe Fairfax High, as well, and ask, "Would you see a film called *Mutant* or *Forbidden World*?" At that time, most people didn't know "mutant" meant. I kept saying, "It's a great film title. They'll understand it." Roger kept insisting on *Forbidden World*, and I said, "People are going to confuse it with *Forbidden Planet* (1956)." He said, "Oh, that one was over twenty years ago, no one will ever remember it." And he changed the artwork from the mutant with slime coming out of it to a girl being raped on a rock by a bug monster that had nothing to do with the movie. So, I had a hard time....

SA: In your estimation, then, the film's not ruined, but it is compromised.

AH: Absolutely. My second agent, Jim Berkus, who represented the Coen brothers, looked at *Forbidden World* and said, "If it were a little bit hipper, I could represent you." I showed him *Mutant* and he said, "Cool." He recognized the difference. He said, "People are going to pick up that you did something interesting here."

SA: Well, it's a bit sad what happened. A sort of *Magnificent Ambersons* (1942) of low-budget sci-fi horror. But at least there is that director's cut out there.

AH: I actually anticipated this sort of thing, so I stole the original, and only, print of the entire *Mutant* from New World. When Roger found out about it, he demanded that I return it. I refused. "If I give it back," I said, "you're going to get rid of it. I don't trust you." Roger is someone who inspires everyone. He's first and foremost a great filmmaker, and what he achieved in his directing career was fantastic. What he did with this achievement and his nurturing of young filmmakers changed the film industry. He was great. But you have to fight him. You have to fight to make your movie. The thing we said more than anything else was "But, Roger—"

SUSAN JUSTIN

Interview by Stephen B. Armstrong

STEPHEN B. ARMSTRONG: How did you get into music and film?

SUSAN JUSTIN: As a really good note reader and pianist, I played piano all through school, accompanying everybody, fifth grade through undergrad. I also sang a lot—both my parents had really nice voices. Right out of high school, I became a foreign exchange student and went to Denmark with American Field Service. I had to choose a line of study and chose music— suddenly I had to learn theory. Then I attended UCLA and received a degree in music. That's how I got my skills for writing. Pretty much everything I learned at UCLA I've used on the job. Half way through undergrad I went back to Denmark for a year and just played piano at the Music Conservatory in Copenhagen. When I wasn't in the practice room I was out singing in the subway, the street and in clubs. Back in L.A., I met Allan Holzman, and he was directing and editing film. Whenever he needed a film score, he would ask, "Can you do this?"

My first big job was the score for *Forbidden World*. I have memories of putting it all down on paper, note for note, even though the recording was done on synthesizers for the most part. That was pre-software. Prior to that, I scored the trailer for Roger Corman's *Firecracker* that Allan edited. I got myself into a little trouble because they wanted something that was like the *Peter Gunn* theme—dee-dee-dee-dee dee-dee-dee-dee DEE-dee—and I changed a few notes. But Roger got caught for getting too close to it, and he had to pay for rights, so he wasn't really pleased with me from the outset; but I still got a few other jobs from him down the line. I did quite a few B movie film scores, mostly on synthesizer. I had a band, so sometimes my bandmates would join me in the studio, or we'd have a couple of soloists here and there, but it was mostly synthesizers.

I was very fortunate to work with Craig Huxley, who had a really nice studio in his house. He was one of the top contracted synth players at the time. What a cool mentor to have! I was also performing a lot in clubs, so vocals became part of the scores, as well. As time went on, I received more and more film scoring opportunities for documentaries. After I had kids, because we lived in an open space, a loft-type space, it was a lot easier to work on documentaries than B-movies.

SA: Where did you grow up?

SJ: I grew up in Arcadia, California, right next to Pasadena and the Santa Anita Racetrack. The school district had a great music department. I was so fortunate to sing and play music every day while in school, K-12.

SA: Did you have an interest in popular music? One of the reasons, Allan explained to me, he wanted you to score *Forbidden World* rather than James Horner, was your ability to write "New Wave" material. But your emphasis seems to have been classical.

SJ: Yes, it was. As soon as I got out of UCLA, people kept asking me: "Can you do this? Can you do that?" This developed into songwriting, and once I got into a songwriting phase, a band was easy to put together. All those skills came together for film scoring. I was very fortunate to participate in the ASCAP and BMI Film Scoring Workshops. Of course, having Allan as a husband on the film scene made it really easy. I still write things for him. That's been a nice collaboration.

SA: Which film score composers and popular musicians have influenced you and shaped your aesthetic.

SJ: Ennio Morricone stands out because he has such great simplicity of melodic invention. He's much more melodic than, say, someone like Jamie Horner—we were at UCLA together—who was more orchestral in his compositional approach. My best skill is coming up with a simple melody. Everything for me starts there, not with orchestration. In terms of pop and rock, I was fascinated with Brian Eno and the synth stuff he was doing—he created a lot of ambient music. Talking Heads was really an inspiration, too. I'm also inspired by some of the current music that is heavily synth realized. It's kind of cool that synth has come back in the last four or five years. After college, I was staff pianist at Santa Monica College for ten years, and I played many musicals. Sitting at the keyboard playing musicals—that's a lot of great melodies going by. I've written my own musical with a TV writer friend of mine. She's a good collaborator and a four-time Emmy-award winner. Actually, I'm sitting and looking at the book as we speak. It's a sci-fi love story.

SA: I had a chance to watch you on YouTube performing the theme from *Forbidden World*.

SJ: Oh, yes.

SA: Pretty neat stuff. Allan in his interview pointed out that he likes the score because it is driving and that it has good melodies in it. Do you recall how you wrote and how you recorded the tracks for the film?

SJ: Well, I had a small keyboard setup at home, but I really composed at the piano. I was just starting out with the synthesizers, but I remember sitting mostly at the piano. In order to take the music into the studio, I wrote everything out. We didn't have the software yet where you can play the keyboard and it comes up on the page. I don't know if I had taken a film score workshop yet. I kind of just figured it out on the fly. Mostly I was trying to have recurring themes for the different characters or the different production sets. Then we got into the studio and I had access to more synthesizers. People didn't really have banks of synthesizers then, but Craig had the big Moog synthesizer and this thing called the Blaster Beam, which was at least fourteen feet long. It was a metal beam he designed, strung with piano wire; a big metal tube that you could drag the length of it made those wires roar. Craig had really cool sound effects in that studio. Some of my friends came in and played. I used my voice a lot. It all came together, and it was really *fun*.

AARON LIPSTADT

Interview by Stephen B. Armstrong

STEPHEN B. ARMSTRONG: I watched *Android* (1982) twice last night.

AARON LIPSTADT: Wow. Good thing it's short.

SA: It's a wonderful little film. I've studied the New World sci-fi pictures closely—*Galaxy of Terror* and *Forbidden World* and so forth. I think the two I enjoy the most must be *Android* and *Forbidden World*. Maybe it's because they're not so violent and grotesque. They're just good stories. Okay, let's start. What led you to the movies?

AL: I got interested in movies at the University of Chicago, which had a very active, very knowledgeable film society. The people there were well-educated and had a lot of experience, a lot of breadth, as many of them had been interested in film since high school. This film society, Doc Films [Documentary Film Group], was and still is the oldest film society in the country. At that time, it was very much comprised of Andrew Sarris acolytes, who were into finding and showing obscure American films, especially genre films. So I came to college and met a group of people who were basically American movie snobs, watching John Ford, Howard Hawks, Edgar Ulmer.... That was the context for my real film education.

The university had virtually no film studies program to speak of. There was one professor, John Cawelti, who'd written a book about Westerns, *The Six-Gun Mystique,* but he was in the English Department. I was there to study political science and international relations and Communist Party systems, planning to go to law school. When I got to my senior year, I had something of a crisis, and I decided at the last minute after taking my GREs and my law boards to attend Northwestern's film department. I contacted the head of the department and said, "I'm interested in enrolling in the Ph.D. program in film studies." He looked at my transcripts and at my grades and gave me a full scholarship. Three months later I was at Northwestern.

The chair of the department at Northwestern, Paddy Whannel, had been head of the Education Department at the British Film Institute. He would periodically bring his colleagues from London. When I was at Northwestern, Geoffrey Nowell-Smith came and so did Peter Wollen from the department of theoretical linguistics at the University of Essex. After two years at Northwestern, I spent a year in London studying with Peter Wollen. Everyone was into what was then a very exciting and popular course of study—using semiotics and linguistics to analyze film structure. My reaction was "Well, here I am in England, and everybody is doing this theoretical semiotics work. I don't want to do what everybody else is doing." So I decided to do my thesis on American movies. Since I had a background in social science and political science and economics, I thought I'd do an analysis of Roger Corman's New World. Roger in interviews had said how he is politically left wing, that he backs the outsider, that his movies are about the counterculture. I thought it would be interesting to apply a political analysis of the content of the movies and an economic analysis of how they were made and distributed to see what kind of contradictions there were.

I completed all my coursework and moved from London to Boston, where I started writing my thesis. I made contact with a woman named Mary Ann Fisher, who was Roger's assistant. She was very helpful in getting me prints—they had a Boston exchange for all the New World movies. I watched pretty much the entire New World output on an upright Moviola in my apartment, which was very trying. Mary Ann also told me she could get me in touch with some New World directors. I finally came out to Los Angeles to meet people and do interviews, and she arranged for me to talk to Roger and some directors—George Armitage and Jonathan Kaplan. I was there, I guess, ten days. Before I left, Mary Ann said, "You should get a job here."

I went back to Boston, and I was writing my thesis and thinking, "Well, what am I going to do after I finish? Where am I going to work? What are the chances I'm getting a teaching job?" At that time there were only three strong departments that were doing academic film work: UCLA, USC and NYU. The chance of getting a job at any of them was pretty slim. It was more likely I'd get a job somewhere like Macalester College or the University of Iowa—Cedar Rapids or the University of Alabama in Huntsville. I didn't know where. It just seemed to me: "Maybe I'm not going to live where I want to live and do what I want to do if I keep going down this road." And I kept hearing this ringing in my ears: "You should get a job here. You should get a job here."

To make a long story short, I called Mary Ann and said, "I'm going to try to find a job. I know there's a possibility I can do this because the Directors Guild has a training program and various agencies have training programs." I gave myself six months. I said, "If a job doesn't happen, I'm going to finish my thesis."

Mary Ann told me that Roger had two assistants. She was the senior assistant and Gale Anne Hurd was the junior assistant. Gale was at that time in northern California working on *Humanoids from the Deep*. Mary Ann said, "You can come down here and do an interview and maybe replace Gale while she is gone." Roger, who went to Stanford, had hired no one but Stanford graduates for the previous ten years, including Mary Ann and Gale.

Somehow Mary Ann only gave him my resume. He'd already met me when I'd interviewed him for the thesis. I think my having been at Northwestern impressed him. And I got the job.

Roger had bought a studio, a lumberyard in Venice, which he was going to make into his production facility. Science fiction pictures were pretty popular then, like they are now, and he was going to make them at this facility. He wouldn't have to worry about sending crews out on location. No worries about weather, either; there'd be more control over the environment. Part of his plan, too, was that he would have a visual effects facility that would service his pictures. He was then in the middle of making his biggest picture, *Battle Beyond the Stars*. The budget for this was pretty high, over $2 million, which for Roger was a big deal. But it was getting into trouble pretty early on. The director was not quite up to the job. The picture was an ambitious remake of *The Magnificent Seven* in outer space, and we had all these characters and a lot of makeup and visual effects. Roger said that I could help if I was down in Venice at the studio. So I was moved there and had my first taste of production.

With Roger, you pretty much get thrown in. You take on responsibility and learn more and more. Or you fail, and you're never heard from again. I kept my eyes open and my mouth shut and learned from the mistakes of other people. I was basically a glorified PA on that movie. But I wasn't one of the PAs who spent the day off in Hollywood picking up equipment and making production runs. I was in the office, where I was learning about scheduling and budgeting. I had a knack for that. With my economics background I was quick with numbers. It came easily to me. Roger had me work with a veteran production manager, which meant overseeing budget and schedule. I did a very short, three-day production. And the next thing you know, I was a production manager. I did that for a couple of pictures, and it worked out pretty well.

SA: Which New World films were you attached to back then?

AL: One of them was *Galaxy of Terror*—that was the first one on which I was production manager. Then *Saturday the 14th* (1982). *Saturday the 14th* was a picture that Roger's wife, Julie, was producing, a parody of *Friday the 13th* (1980). I was on that for just a couple weeks. I produced the second unit, if I remember correctly. Around that time, I found out about an unproduced script Roger had. I should mention that Roger had a script development person, a very capable, very talented person named Frances Doel. She passed me the script, which Roger owned, that became *Slumber Party Massacre*, although it was filmed under the title *Sleepless Night*, a much more benign title. The script was by a pretty well-known feminist author, Rita Mae Brown, who'd written an acclaimed novel, *Rubyfruit Jungle*. There were no plans at that point to make this picture, but Frances had given the script to a young, talented editor named Amy Jones, who wanted to direct. On her own, Amy produced and directed a five-page prologue for *Slumber Party Massacre* and showed this to Roger. Needless to say, he was impressed—by the quality of the work and that Amy had the balls to go out and do this—and that she spent her own money to make this five-minute teaser for this movie, which was helped no doubt by the fact that her husband, Michael Chapman, was cinematographer. You probably know that Michael Chapman is now a multi-Academy-Award-nominated cinematographer. It looked great, so Roger said she could make this movie. But his idea was that they would make it super-cheap. I think he wanted to do it for $200 thousand. Amy was probably in her late twenties or early thirties, but she looked like a teenager. Roger's idea was that they were going to pretend it was a student film. No union, no IA, no SAG, no DGA. Nothing. Normally, Roger made all his movies non-union anyway, except he did use SAG actors. In this case, he wasn't even using SAG actors.

I got wind of this, and I went and met Amy. I said, "I understand you're going to make this movie with Roger, and I want to be your producer." Amy said, "Great." I tried this on Roger, but he'd already picked a young Stanford woman to be the producer. *Slumber Party Massacre* basically takes place in a big house, so Roger had told this producer to go to the set of *Saturday the*

14th, which was shooting at that time, because that picture was also taking place in a big house. Roger told the producer, "Look through the location pictures the *Saturday the 14th* people put together to help you get a head start on finding the house for your movie." she was down there with the production crew at this big old house in Los Angeles near USC, looking through photos. Then Roger called for Julie, who, as I mentioned, was producing *Saturday the 14th*. He called on a landline phone, of course, and someone then went to get Julie, without being able to put Roger on hold. Meanwhile, this producer was looking through the location photos. Someone says to her, "What are you doing?" "Well, I'm looking for locations for this shitty horror movie I'm producing." Roger's on the phone three feet away, hears her say this, promptly fires her and hires me to produce the picture.

So now I'm a New World Pictures producer, and the next picture we are making is a picture another editor is going to direct. Roger really liked hiring editors because they were always sure to get enough coverage because they knew what they'd need in the editing room. This editor, Allan Holzman, had already worked for Roger on a couple pictures. We were now working on *Galaxy of Terror* together We started on a Wednesday, and Roger comes by the first day. We had this big spaceship control-room/pilot's room set, and Roger asks about costs and schedule for this set, which we planned to strike, dismantle and remove over the weekend. But Roger told us, "Don't strike the set." He then goes to the editing room, where Allan is working, and says, "If you can write an opening to a science fiction picture where a guy crash lands on a planet, we can shoot it this weekend on these sets and then make the rest of the movie later." Allan writes this script, which became to the opening for *Forbidden World*, in two days about a guy in space. A computer wakes him up. The ship crashes. The set was then repainted, and this thing was shot over the weekend. We got an actor, Jesse Vint, who was sort of a low-budget leading man at the time. The idea was that later they would write the rest of the script and shoot the movie on location, where the ship has crashed.

So after *Galaxy of Terror*, *Saturday the 14th* and *Slumber Party Massacre*, the next picture was going to be *Forbidden World*, and Allan, the director, asked me to shoot second unit. I think partly this is because we were sort of friends and partly because he thought that if I were directing second unit I'd be more invested in the movie than strictly as a producer, and maybe I would give him a little more slack and more resources, which was true in a way. So I started directing second unit. I was pretty terrible at it, mostly because it was a lot of insert stuff. Allan, as an editor, knew exactly what he wanted to do with this material, and I, as a producer, really didn't. But I got the hang of it. And as Allan got a little behind, I started getting more stuff to do, working with actors. One day Allan says to me, "Can you get some sort of spooky hallway stuff with the actor creeping down the hallway?" I get the actor. We shoot for a couple hours. Then someone says to me, "We need you on the main unit." Then the actor says to me, "How long you been doing this?" "What?" I say. He says, "Directing." I look at my watch. "Since about noon." I'm wondering what he's going to say because this is the first time I'm directing an actor. He says, "Because you're better at it than the other guy." That kind of knocked my socks off because I'd been thinking, "Here I am working for Roger Corman. I'm on the producing track with Roger, so I'm probably going to become a producer."

Then I'm thinking: "Well, maybe I can be a director. Amy Jones shoots a five-minute opening and gets to make her movie. Allan Holzman writes a teaser and gets to shoot the opening to his movie, and then he gets to make his movie. Maybe this is the place where we can get our shot." I go to Roger and say, "I'm interested in directing a movie." He's kind of amused, but he tells me that he's going to have me write a script, and if he likes it, I can direct it. The script was going to be called *Alien Sex Shocker*—that's the working title. It was to be about aliens who abduct women for reproductive experiments. I am dismayed. "Oh, God, this was not what I had in mind. I wanted to do *The Godfather* (1972), and he's got me doing *Alien Sex Shocker*." And then I had the idea, which I thought was brilliant, of setting the Patty Hearst story in outer space. I actually started writing that.

Meanwhile, there were two carpenters, James Reigle and Don Opper, who worked for Roger and had written a script. They know that I'm interested in directing, that I directed second unit on *Forbidden World*, and that Roger told me that if he liked my script, then I could direct. They came to me and said, "Why don't you think about directing our script?" I read it, and it's really pretty good. They have relatives in Chicago, who have some money. They go to the people in Chicago and say, "We're making this movie for Roger Corman for half-a-million dollars. If you put up half of it, you'll own half of it." Then the writers go to Roger and say, "We've got these guys in Chicago itching to spend money, and they want to make a movie. Here's the script. Put up half the money, and we can make this movie. Roger, what do you say?"

Now Roger, being a good businessman, would put up part of his quarter-million dollars in studio and equipment because he owned his cameras, his own lights, his own studio. His cash out is going to be minimal. He gets U.S. distribution. The guys in Chicago get foreign. One of the writers, Don Opper, wanted to play the lead in the movie. He'd basically written the role for himself. Eventually we get the Chicago people to commit the money. But Roger is very leery about having the writer be the actor: he's not going to want to change things; he's not going to be able to take direction because he's the writer. But eventually Roger agrees. So, Don Opper, the co-writer, plays the lead in this movie, which is called *Android*. It's my first movie to direct, and we made that for twenty days, nineteen of which were done at Venice in the lumberyard and one day on location. That's how I started directing

SA: New World eventually sold off its investment in the film? Is that right? What I understand is that SHO Films bought out Roger's share?

AL: We made the movie, and it came out better than we expected. We were pretty happy with it. But Roger set up a screening in Spokane, and apparently it did not go so well. *Android* was clearly not a Roger movie. It had zero sex and very little violence. The main star was a European arthouse actor, Klaus Kinski, whom no one had heard of. He wasn't quite sure what to do with it, or what he had on his hands. In fact, when we had the opportunity to get the script to Kinski to play the villain in the movie, Roger had been

194

completely uninterested. The way it worked out with SHO was this: Roger at New World had U.S. distribution, and the Chicago investors owned foreign distribution. The Chicago investors realized Klaus Kinski would be a good name for foreign distribution in Europe and South America. They had put up the money for the overage we needed to get Klaus. We finished the movie in I think it was September or October of 1982. We started trying to get into film festivals because we were either optimistic or naive or crazy. I'll never forget the rejection we got from the New York Film Festival, which was extremely condescending. But we did get into the London Film Festival, which was a pretty big deal. I went to London for that; it was just incredible—a Saturday night in a twelve-hundred-seat theater—Queen Elizabeth's Hall. There was an incredibly positive reaction. The people who owned foreign said, "Roger doesn't know what to do with this movie, but we have a sleeper here." They decided to put up the money and buy Roger out. This company, SHO Films, was basically the producers'—Don's brother, Barry, Rupert Harvey and Fred Schwartz, who was the money man from Chicago. Don and I were junior partners.

SA: Klaus Kinski had come from Werner Herzog's *Fitzcarraldo*, and now he was working with you on a low-budget sci-fi. How was he to direct?

AL: It's not like he was George Clooney or Brigitte Bardot or Elizabeth Taylor—he wasn't a big star. But he was a big star in his own mind and a big star in Werner Herzog's movies. He agreed to do *Android*, he'd said, because he thought it would be fun for his son, who was five or six at the time, to see him do this character in a science fiction movie, and it would be more accessible than *Fitzcarraldo*. It was going to be two weeks work for him. He'd come down to L.A. We were excited. For us, Klaus Kinski was not just as an actor, he was an iconic figure. The rest of the cast was fairly small, just five or six people: Don had written it; the other actors had done more theater and not much with movies or didn't have much experience at all; the female lead, Brie Howard, was not really an actress—I'd seen her in a rock band and

195

thought she'd be interesting. Klaus was a different beast. We were a little worried. We were slightly concerned about how to keep him focused. We'd heard rumors from *Fitzcarraldo* that he was a ladies' man and easily distracted, so part of our plan was to keep the women PAs around him and lead him around. I don't know if that was successful or not, but nobody got hurt.

I remember vividly that we started shooting before Klaus showed up. His first scene comes after these space bandit refugees, these runaway criminals, have done their emergency landing at his space station when he first goes to meet them. This was the first scene we filmed with him, and the actors were extremely excited about rehearsing with Klaus. he came to the set. Everybody meets. I set the scene, and it's time to rehearse. Klaus walks out of the elevator into the room. He says, "So, I walk up here and blah-blah-blah. And I turn around and go back." Everybody's a little like *okay*. I say, "Great. Let's try that again." He does it again. "I come out here. Blah-blah-blah. And I walk back." The actors, who'd been waiting for their chance to rehearse with Klaus, responded as if they'd been poleaxed. They couldn't believe this was his rehearsal technique. I said, "Okay. Great." We mark it, we light it, we start shooting. And all of a sudden out comes Klaus, and now he's all charisma. You can't keep your eyes off him. He turned it all on once the cameras were rolling. That was a revelation for me. For a first-time director trying to understand how to deal with this range of people, it was a great learning experience.

Bibliography

Brock, Jason V. "Roger Corman: Socially Conscious Auteur." *Disorders of Magnitude: A Survey of Dark Fantasy*, edited by Jason V. Brock, 95-100. Rowman & Littlefield, 2014.

Chute, David. "The New World of Roger Corman." *Film Comment*, vol. 18, no. 2, 1982, pp. 27-32.

Corman, Roger, with Jim Jerome. *How I Made a Hundred Movies in Hollywood and Never Lost a Dime*. Random House, 1990.

Corman's World: Exploits of a Hollywood Rebel. Directed by Alex Stapleton, A&E Indiefilms, 2011.

Di Franco, J. Philip. *The Movie World of Roger Corman*. Chelsea House, 1979.

Dixon, Winston Wheeler. "Roger Corman." *Contemporary North American Film Directors: A Wallflower Critical Guide*, edited by Yorah Alom, et al. pp. 104-107. Wallflower Press, 2002.

Gray, Beverly. "Lessons from the Roger Corman School of Moviemaking." *MovieMaker*, Spring 2001, p. 48.

—-. *Roger Corman: An Unauthorized Biography of the Godfather of Indie Filmmaking*. Renaissance, 2000.

Gregory, Mollie. *Women Who Run the Show: How a Brilliant and Creative New Generation of Women Stormed Hollywood*. St. Martin's Press, 2002, p. 146.

Heffernan, Nick. "No Parents, No Church, No Authorities in Our Films: Exploitation Movies, The Youth Audience, and Roger Corman's Counterculture Trilogy." *Journal of Film and Video*. 67.2, Summer 2015, pp. 3-20.

Kapsis, Robert E. *Hitchcock: The Making of a Reputation*. University of Chicago Press, 1992.

Kehr, Dave. "Four Auteurs in Search of an Audience." *Film Comment*, Sept-Oct, 1977, pp. 6-15.

Koetting, Christopher T. *Mind Warp: The Fantastic True Story of Roger Corman's New World Pictures*. Midnight Marquee, 2013.

Machete Maidens Unleashed! Directed by Mark Hartley, Bionic Boy Productions, 2010.

McGee, Mark Thomas. *Roger Corman, The Best of the Cheap Acts*. McFarland, 1988.

Naha, Ed. *The Films of Roger Corman: Brilliance on Budget*. Arco, 1982.

Nashawaty, Chris. *Crab Monsters, Teenage Cavemen, and Candy Stripe Nurses: Roger Corman:*

King of the B Movie. Harry N. Adams, 2013.

Nasr, Constantine (ed.), *Roger Corman: Interviews*. Univ. Press of Mississippi, 2011.

Lipstadt, Aaron, and Jim Hillier. *Roger Corman's New World. BFI Dossier 7*. British Film Institute, 1981.

Roger Corman: Hollywood's Wild Angel. Directed by Christian Blackwood, Blackwood Productions, 1978.

Silver, Alain, and James Ursini. *Roger Corman: Metaphysics on a Shoestring*. Silman-James, 2006.

Villepique, Greg. "Roger Corman." *Salon*. 13 June, 2000.

Waddell, Calum. *Jack Hill: The Exploitation and Blaxploitation Master, Film by Film*. McFarland, 2008.

Index

201

Notes on the Contributors

Stephen B. Armstrong's writing has appeared in *Film Quarterly, Film Score Monthly, Classic Images, Filmfax*, the *Journal of Popular Culture, Journal of American Culture, Journal of the Utah Academy, Crime Time, Mystery Scene* and *South Atlantic Review*. Armstrong is the author of *Pictures about Extremes: The Films of John Frankenheimer* (McFarland, 2008), *Andrew V. McLaglen: The Life and Hollywood Career* (McFarland, 2011) and *Paul Bartel: The Life and Films* (McFarland, 2017). He edited John Frankenheimer: Interviews, Essays & Profiles (Scarecrow, 2013). A professor of English, he teaches in the Creative Writing and Professional & Technical Writing emphases at Dixie State University in St. George, Utah. Most recently, he edited the literary portions of film director Steve Carver's coffee table book, *Western Portraits: The Unsung Heroes & Villains of the Silver Screen* (Olms, 2019). Armstrong earned his Ph.D. in English (Creative Writing) from Florida State University in 2004.

Madison Bidinger graduated in May 2019 from Dixie State University with a degree in English (Professional & Technical Writing—*summa cum laude*). A member of Sigma Tau Delta, the International English Honor Society, she has presented her research at the Utah Conference of Undergraduate Research and the Dixie State University Research Symposium. Her writing has appeared in *St. George Health & Wellness*, and she served as an editor for DSU's literary publications, the *Southern Quill* and *Route 7 Review*.

Randy Jasmine is a professor of English at Dixie State University in St. George, Utah, where he teaches a variety of composition and literature courses. He earned his Ph.D. from the University of Mississippi. His research interests include Charles Dickens, George Gissing, African American literature, Southern literature and popular culture.

Krista Kirkham graduated *summa cum laude* from Dixie State University in May 2019. She received a B.S. in English with an emphasis in Creative Writing. She was the Creative Writing Student of the Semester in the fall of 2018 and was nominated for The Dixie 11 Award and as Student of the Year. She was the 2018-2019 managing editor for *The Southern Quill*. Her writing has been published in *The Southern Quill*, the *Dixie State University Academic Report 2019*, *The Independent* (St. George, Utah) and *The Dollhouse*. Her short story "Kiss in the Dust" received the 2019 Naythan M. Bell fiction award. Following graduation, she moved to Salt Lake City, where she now works as a freelance writer.

William Nesbitt, Ph.D., is a professor of English at Beacon College in Leesburg, Florida. His articles, creative writing, reviews and interviews have appeared in *Aja*, *Manzano Mountain Review*, *One Person's Trash: A Literary Journal*, *Angry Old Man Magazine: Experimental Art and Poetry*, *Beat Drama: Playwrights and Performances of the 'Howl' Generation*, *Beatdom*, *Route 7 Review*, *Popular Culture Review*, *Kudzu House Quarterly*, the *Southeast Review* and the *Journal of Evolutionary Psychology*. His books include *Teaching Students with Learning Disabilities at Beacon College: Lessons from the Inside* (Lang, 2017). He is the editor of the forthcoming *Forsaken: The Making and Aftermath of Roger Corman's The Fantastic Four* (BearManor). He has numerous music reviews, musician interviews and articles about music circulating online.

Robert Powell is an assistant professor of English at Alabama A&M. He earned his Ph.D. in English from Florida State University in 2006 (dissertation: *Ayn Rand's Heroes: Between and Beyond Good and Evil*). He is a veteran, having served in the United States Marine Corps Reserve. Robert enjoys shooting pool, playing video games and traveling to favorite summer destinations with his wife, Felicia.

Amy Whiting is a student at Dixie State University, pursuing her degree in English. She is new to writing and editing and has enjoyed learning from her professors and peers. Amy knows that she is just scratching the surface of what makes up the English language and how to make a piece of work shine. In the future, she hopes to be a published author of her own books.

Lightning Source UK Ltd.
Milton Keynes UK
UKHW020805160620
364898UK00003B/150